DR. MAGIC

SIX

ONE ACT PLAYS

JOYCE CAROL OATES

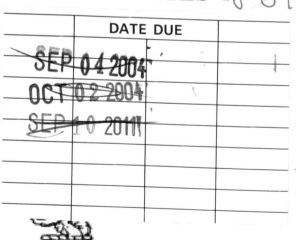
SAMUEL FRENCH, INC.

45 West 52th Street
NEW YORK 10010
LONDON

7623 Sunset Boulevard
HOLLYWOOD 90046
TORONTO

IMPORTANT BILLING AND CREDIT REQUIREMENTS

CONTENTS

HOMESICK

HOMESICK was first performed at McCarter Theatre, Princeton, 1995.

CAST

PINKTOES: *A young Caucasian woman, 20*
MR. AMERICA: *Caucasian male, mid-30's*

SETTING: *Rural Texas*
TIME: *Hallowe'en morning*

(LIGHTS UP. A young woman wrapped loosely in a coarse stained blanket, bare-legged, wearing only bloodstained pink wool socks, addresses the audience.)

PINKTOES. *(Childlike hurt, reproach)*Momma—! *(Pause)* You see what's happened to me...it's your fault. *(Pause)* Wouldn't never of left home if...you know...you needed to love me better *(Angrily wipes at eyes)* Now, nobody even knows what I am. where I'm ending up. "Roscommon, Texas." Never heard of it before! Damn long way from home... *(Pause, accusing)* JANE DOE "PINKTOES" is my name here—that's all they know me by. 'Cause all I'm wearing, the Texas cops find me, is these old socks Grandma knitted for me. *(Indicates socks)* Ugh! How'd they get so...dirty? *(Stares at bloodstains; pause; shift tone)* Hey, I remember opening my Christmas present from Grandma...how pretty the socks was. She'd been knitting them for me in secret not letting me know. *(Pause)* How long ago was that? I guess...a long time? *(Pause)* It's easy to forget, on the road...always moving...no place you are. *(Figures it out)* Yeah, O.K.: been gone from home four years. In December. It's Hallowe en morning now, I ain't gonna get to December this year. *(Pause)* Momma, you listening? *(Stares into audience, hurt and accusing)* Naw, you ain't. I know.

(LIGHTS DIM on PINKTOES. LIGHTS UP on MR. AMERICA, a man in his mid-thirties, husky, handsome, in cheaply stylish but not new clothes; hair slickly oiled, a two- or three-days' growth of beard.)

MR. AMERICA. *(Proudly, an air of reverence)* First time, I was five years old. Ashland, West Virginia where I was born. My Momma run me out of the trailer 'cause she was...entertaining a guest...so I was down by the creek bank and it was dark and I looked and saw this...fire!...this Burning Bush... except it was going along the ground like a wheel. I was so scared almost pissed my pants! The Lord God giving me a sign! It came at me and I tried to catch it in my hand...rolling whoosh! along the ground. *(Demonstrates)* Oh! my fingers was burnt and blistered but I didn't feel no pain, I was struck down where I stood. And Momma next morning finds me sleeping under the trailer

7

my hands so hurt like they was— *(He shows his scarred palms to the audience)* —she was repentant like a sinner called to judgment. *(Pause, dreamy)* Momma's hair like corn tassels and her face a shining light... *(Pause, Self-condemning, repressed anger)* There is a ministry of Love, and there is a ministry of Hurt. I know I was born to preach the Love not practice the Hurt and how—this came to be— *(By "this" meaning his identity as a killer)* — before the Lord Jesus I don't comprehend. *(Defensive)* "Pinktoes"?—who? When's this? *(Pause)* There's so many of them! And the pictures of them where they don't look nothing like who they were exactly but like others of them—females. *(Pause, muddled in his words)* I mean—you 'em they're s'post to be...you'd be fucked, too. *(Pause)* letting me go. *(Slicks back his hair, looking "innocent")* I'd tell 'em, "No sir, no ma'am, not me, I'm a good boy washed in the Blood of the Lamb, not me." *(Wide innocent mock-smile)* Union card in my wallet. *(Slaps pocket)* I look like anybody's boy cousin, eh? If I was a nigger, that'd be a different story! *(Laughs. More somber, matter-of-fact)* Well—maybe I remember. Yeah. This Li'l girl all alone. Looking kind of sad, strung-out. My eye drawn to her by the will of the Lord—them pink socks she was wearing. I'm thinking, Is it a sign? O Lord, a sign from You? Truck-stop on I-35, Oklahoma. Headed south to Texas. *(Becoming more impassioned)* The sky all afire where the sun was going down, a long long time setting so my eyes was seared, I took that for a sign. *(In Biblical cadences)* So he drove out the man; and he placed at the east of the garden of Eden Cherubims, and a flaming sword which turned every way, to keep the way of the tree of life. *(Pause shakes head as if to clear it)* She was alone at one of them picnic tables in the dusk...she'd been crying, her pretty face all puffy and eyes red so I was drawn to her as to a sister. *(MR. AMERICA and PINKTOES glance at each other, shyly.)* A poor lost soul needing help! Told her I'd buy us some Kentucky Fried chicken, and a six-pack of Coor's, she looked like she was starving. And me, too. But not right here, I said, this ain't the place, I said. So I got her my car and we drove off...how many hours, I don't know. She was asleep going into Texas, her head on my shoulder...*(Pause.)* I accept my fate, it's no choice for a reaonable man. I know there is God but He is far away.

(LIGHTS DIM on MR. AMERICA LIGHTS UP on PINKTOES.)

PINKTOES. *(Voice rises to a faint scream.)* I DON'T REMEMBER HIS FACE, I COULDN'T IDENTIFY HIM! Just these tattoos up an down his arms... mark of Satan. *(Pause, shakes head.)* Yeah, I believed him. There's been so many of 'em...mostly, they're O.K. You got no choice, sometimes, you're that hungry... strung-out. Damm ol' stomach growling, so hungry...I was embar-

HOMESICK

rassed he'd hear. Yeah and I'm so...dirty. Just don't know how I got so dirty... it ain't my true self. Yeah I asked him could I take a bath...wanted to wash my hair. He said sure! he'd rent us a motel room...like brother and sister, he said. *(Shakes head. self-accusing.)* Shit! Did I believe him? Guess I did... Funny how you're in your body so you understand it's just this kind of...vehicle... God gave you to use. Right? Where the spirit abides. *(Sings)* "This little light of mine, I'm gonna let it shine... Let it shine all over God's moun-tain, I'm gonna let it shine... *(Voice trails off)* Grandma taught me that. *(Pause)* Once you're dead, though, in folks' eyes, the body is all you are. And strangers not even knowing your name. *(Dreamy)* Grandma called me "honey" Picked me her favorite to spite the rest of them. She'd say, "You're my girl, honey, ain't you?" If Momma yelled at me, or slapped... 'Cause I was a little slow through grammar school. Because I'd run off and hide. I loved Grandma and she loved me. Because I was the one to help Grandma wash her long hair, that she was so proud she never cut all her life. Real pretty silvery hair— long, to here! *(Indicates her waist)* "Your grandpa made me promise I'd never cut my hair, so I never did. Isn't that something?—sixty years back. And him dead since 1941"*(Pause)* And I'd wash Grandma's feet for her where she was too stout to bend. And clip her toenails, and bunions all grown over like scabs. She had all these..what day a call em... geraniums, in pots...I'd help her with. *(Pause)* Could be, Grandma's dead now. I don't think about it. *(Pause)* Momma said I sure didn't take after her. Yeah I hated my sisters— so pretty-pretty! You get your way if you're pretty-pretty like on TV or in the movies so if you're not, learn to make your own way. *(Belligerent)* Started in, age thirteen, I wouldn't take none of their shit no longer. When I threw my plate on the floor, yeah I'd go hungry but they caught on to respect me. When I shouted, I sure didn't stammer.

(LIGHTS DIM on PINKTOES. LIGHTS UP on MR. AMERICA.)

MR. AMERICA. Huh! It's these "court-appointed" thr'pists as they call themselves, and the lawyers—nothing but a game with them, they don't give a shit. And the "doctors"—hoo, that's a laugh!—these jerk-offs at Plainfield couldn't speak English nor comprehend it. Dark enough to be niggers but not—one of 'em wearing a fucking turban. *(Indicating his own head with a winding motion; derisive)* Them saying I suffer from "temporal lobe trauma"— lead and "cadmium toxins"—from when I was a kid. Momma banged me around some, and Momma's men friends—O.K. But that's a long time ago. *(Pause, reminiscing)* This one time my mother was gone. went off with somebody...I hid out in the woods...getting stuff to eat out of garbage cans, dumpsters...

HOMESICK

one night, a guy took a shot at me with a .22, told me to get the hell out what'd I think I was, a fucking raccoon? *(Laughs, ironic.)* Yes, and Jesus saying, "Light is come into the world—!" *(Urgent, matter-of-fact.)* There was this woman turned up in Blacksburg. Where we was then with one of Momma's man friends. She was slow-witted you could see. Said she would have sex with me then changed her mind seeing something in my face. She was a dirty whore. She was cross-eyed. She was the one I blame. *(Pause.)* In a field beyond the old train yard there's oil drums, freight cars...she started fighting me screaming so I got pissed— *(Strangling motions with hands.)* —shut her up good! Whore! Then I fucked her—good! Two, three times! Dragged some tarpaulin over her so nobody'd see then I went home to Mr. Cady's where Momma was "house- keeper"...I was fifteen years old. He was going to send me to Bible College, said he detected the fire of the Lord in my eye. He was in a wheelchair, poor old bastard. Momma'd get drunk and laugh saying all he had was a— *(Gesturing at his crotch.)* —old limp rubbery carrot. *(Laughs sadly.)* They was going to get married but some folks of his fucked up the plans. *(Pause.)* There was school there but I didn't go. I'd make myself wait then go back to the train yard and every time I'd think there's nothing there, naw—and every time she was still there under the tarpaulin. And nobody knew! And nobody was going to know! *(Pause, breathing swiftly.)* I'd get excited...I'd...yeah I'd screw her...couldn't stop myself. *(A moment's anguish; pause.)* They don't judge you in that state. *(Pause.)* *(A beat. MR. AMERICA hides his face, sways, abrupt anger, dropping his hands.)* Huh! I know you're thinking you are SUPERIOR to me. BETTER EDUCATED and BETTER BACK-ground, huh! BETTER NOURISHED in your mother's womb and your mother wasn't no PROSTITUTE. *(Spitting gesture.)* Well, fuck that! *(Evangelical voice.)* "For unto every one that hath shall be given, and he shall have abundance: but from him that hath not shall be taken away even that which he hath." *(Pause.)* Think I don't know that? A man like me don't know that? God give me His sign, I am of the ministry of hurt. *(Rolls up his left sleeve to reveal a lewd crimson flame tattooed on his bicep.)* Take heed: all through this United States of America there's those of us recognize each other by His sign. No matter how far from home we are—we are home.

(LIGHT DIM on MR. AMERICA. LIGHT UP on PINKTOES..)

PINKTOES. *(Defensive.)* Naw, I never knew any of them other girls—s'post to be, what?—twenty-two!—that's been killed along I-35. If it was the same guy or some other bastard been killing 'em. *(Bitter satisfaction.)* Their Mommas feeling like shit, too, eh? *(Strides about in the blanket, almost preening.)*

HOMESICK

Why didn't I go to no shelter in Kansas City?— cause I didn't want to. That's why. Assholes telling me what to do. *(Pause.)* It's O.K. if you're sick, or feeble-minded, which ain't me. I like my independence. It's the open road, for me. *(Pause.)* Yeah I should've sent some cards home—postcards. Fartherest west I was was the Grand Canyon once, and Salt Lake City, with some guy. Should've sent a Christmas card to Grandma, but I didn't. Now...it's too late *(Pause.)* Just as well, Grandma probably ain't alive. She'd feel bad if she knew. *(Considers her body, inside the blanket.)* Jesus! How'd I get all these scars— scabs—bruises—bites and so damn skinny, my ribs showing, collarbone— ninety pounds, about, at the end. You sure got no secrets from the coroner, eh? *(Wry laugh.)* Some of the injuries fresh and some of 'em years old. Like this weird rip like a zipper, here— *(Indicates her left thigh.)* Cut myself up running from a cop—behind a 7-Eleven store in Tulsa-ran into some barbed wire—bleeding like a stuck pig in the back of the squad car and the cops disgusted with me... *(Pause.)* Been pregnant one time, and lost it. The coroner picked up on that. Can't hide nothing from them...bastards V.D., too, it says on the record—"herpes." *(Mispronounces.)* The only jewelry on the "cadaver" is this little jade cross on a gold chain around my neck. *(Indicates necklace, on a thin chain.)* Except it wasn't real jade some guy gave me, and it sure wasn't real gold. Anybody'd guess that, seeing me dumped there dead in the weeds like a tossed-away beer bottle. Dirty pink socks is all I'm wearing. Yeah my stomach's empty. Just Coke he bought me at the rest-stop. Never did get that Kentucky Fried chicken he promised or the Coor's. Fucker!

(LIGHTS UP on MR. AMERICA.)

MR. AMERICA. *(Incensed.)* She was a Christian girl—I thought. Wearing a little cross around her neck. Poor sad child in the pink socks. So far from home, she said, she'd about forgot where was her home. I asked her was she lost and she said she ain't ever been lost. I asked her were her folks missing her at that very moment and she said No! nobody was missing her! ever! but she started crying...poor sad child. *(Pause; now reflective.)* oh God how she was hoping to get a bath, she said. Wash out some of her dirty clothes. Her pink socks—been wearing them so long. At first she seemed kind of scared of me, but interested like they are. Saying, Mister, I'm so tired, I'm by myself, I'm hungry—you got anything to eat? I sure took pity on her from the first sight. That's the tender kind can break your heart—if you let them. *(Sadly.)* I miss my home, too. My momma that was always moving around. But where she was, that was home. If I could get there... I could be washed in the Blood of the Lamb. Momma hoped to make amends, her cousin was Reverend Willy Robbins baptizd me and her together...we were happy, then. For how long I don't know but we were happy and nobody came between us... *(Pause, shakes head.)* At BATON ROUGE they said it was "delusions"—these things I told them they didn't want to believe. "Frontal lobe epilepsy"— so they give me these hot-stinging shots in the ass. Thorazine—that'll make you into a walking zombie. How I escaped?—I walked right out. Work-duty in the laundry and the laundry truck comes in, and the gates are open, and—I walk right out. Hoo! *(Continuing, matter-of-fact.)* I was driving down to Galveston where there was the promise of a job. Oil rig. I'm a good worker, I keep my nose clean I don't cause trouble. Any man knows he can trust me. Long as I'm not drinking. So any judge I come before, there's these "character references" and they're impressed. Never yet had a jury trial, nor wanted one. I told the police all I could remember but it was like a shadow—you can say, sure this is a "human being"but it don't seem so. There isn't the weight, or the—what you call it— *(Rubs thumb and forefinger together.)* —the thickness—texture. The actual killing, when it happens, it's like the shadow is there and a flame flies up over it and that is the flame of Death. *(Pause.)* I have been a witness from, say, twenty feet away. This last time, they were in a drainage ditch, and I was up on a bridge. I saw— but if I blinked, or shut my eyes, it wasn't there. It ceased to exist. *(Contemplative.)* You learn to accept your fate. You bow your head. *(Sings, a tentative, flat, yet yearning voice.)* "Jesus meek and Jesus mild, Jesus became a little child..." Amen! *(Pause.)* Couple years ago in Blacksburg in the psych'ric hospital I visited momma at last. This fat bald bull dog-woman I wouldna know! Momma, I said, I was near to crying, oh Momma you used to be so pretty! and she said, So did you, and laughed. She said, Yeah, my yellow hair fell out one day I wasn't looking. *(Laughs.)* Momma always had a sense of humor. These guys beating on her, and stealing from her and she could take it long as there was food to eat and clothes for me, I was her baby she nursed me at her breast. In the visitors' room right on that filthy floor we prayed together on our knees. I could see she would die soon, they had pumped her so full of poison she was like a waterlogged corpse, and one of her eyes filmed over. She says, May God forgive me, son, that night I got drunk and burnt your hands, held your baby hands in the kerosene stove, and I was crying no matter who was watching me, I said, Oh Momma, that never happened, there's no need to be forgiven. She said, Son. that did happen, not once but many times,see these scars— *(He lifts his hands to contemplate the palms, turns them outward to the audience.)* I said NO MOMMA THESE ARE FROM GOD. These are a sign from God to me, and He has sent others. *(Pause, bitter.)* Damn Ol' senile woman!Bitch! WHORE! *(Regaining control, an air of regret.)* This girl last week, in the pink socks—that was the one I saw, I whispered,

HOMESICK

"Sweet Jesus, let me love her." You want to offer your soul to somebody. You want to do some fucking GOOD in the world. We drove all night and the morning sky was like fire inside the clouds where there was God's face if you had eyes to see. *(Hiding his eyes.)* A sheet of fire washed over the car, the hood all blinding... I was hurt all over my skin like...like lye...like a time I hoped to purify myself rubbing myself with lye...and there was a bridge we drove over exiting from the interstate, and a drainage ditch all dry...big cracks in the earth, and the earth so red...like Mars. That far away! *(MR. AMERICA and PINKTOES glance at each other, as before.)*

(LIGHTS DIM on MR. AMERICA. LIGHTS UP on PINKTOES.)

PINKTOES. That far away! Everything's so far... *(Pause.)* I saw his face but it was blasted in fire. I heard this hard voice out of the underside of the world...no human voice. *(Pause.)*Help me, Jesus, help us who can't help ourselves!... *(Pause.)* Naw. It ain't like that. It's just you. Nobody to help 'cause nobody to witness. *(Pause.)* Raped me, and strangled me, and battered my head till blood leaked out my ears, nose and mouth like a burst tomato. Tore off all my clothes except my socks, he left. That's how the Texas cops find me Hallowe'en morning, driving out patrolling "Devil's Night" damage. This naked dead girl sprawled face down in the weeds in a drainage ditch. Ten yards from the highway. I'm dying maybe three, four hours hearing traffic pass...like thunder... God telling me how bad I was...runaway from O.K. see what happens! what you deserve... *(Pause.)* Texas Intestate I-35 two miles east of Roscommon. Where I'd never been, had no connection with. I-35 runs from Salina, Kansas to Laredo, Texas on the Mexican border—750 miles. Long stretches just empty, desolate like the moon, Where you find us, it's never where we're from—omly where we're dumped. *(Pause.)* "Caucasian female" the cops radioed in. "Caucasian"—that's what I am? *(Pause.)* Said I'd been "good-looking," too. *(Laughs.)* Maybe that's what the cops always say, out of pity? Like, y'know, they got their own sisters, daughters. They try to put the best light on it. *(Pause.)*

(LIGHTS UP on MR. AMERICA, who may be addressing PINKTOES.)

MR. AMERICA. *(Appealing, initially almost boyish.)* Listen, Jesus as my witness, I never meant harm. I am born of the ministry of Love—not Hurt. I meant to get that fried chicken... that six-pack of Coor's... Don't know what, what happened... See, I never counted but they told me, of my thirty-seven years I have been in-car-cer-ated fifteen. Going back to Boys' Home when

HOMESICK

Momma had to give me up for a while. It's O.K. inside. It's what you know. Six A.M. the bell goes and you get up and wash. Six-fifteen a bell goes and you step out, of your cell and march off to mess hall and eat and you're hungry— say it's cereal, it's toast, it's canned peaches or something—it tastes real good. And coffee! O.K. then you march out of mess hall dropping your spoon and fork in a bucket a guard's holding. Your march to your work duty say it's custodian, or grounds, or tag shop where you dip license plates in paint. O.K., nine-thirty A.M. the bell goes and you can smoke. A bell goes and you get back to work. Eleven-thirty, bell goes again you stop work, wash up, march back to your cellhouse. Twelve noon, bell rings and you march to mess hall where you eat, and Jesus you're hungry—it might be meatloaf, fried potatoes, cornbread.*(Smacks Lips.)* Twelve-thirty a bell goes and you march out dropping your spoon, fork in a bucket a guard's holding. You return to work duty. At three P.M. a bell goes and you can smoke. A bell goes and you get back to work. Four-thirty a bell goes and you can wash and march back to your cellhouse. Five o'clock a bell goes and you march to supper. Five-thirty a bell goes and you march to your cellhouse for the night. *(Pause.)* You can pray on your kness long hours. You can read if your eyes don't upset you. There's noise in the cellhouse like in the world but in your cell there's peace. In Boys' Home they beat me and fucked me up the ass, made me their slave, O.K. but that ain't now, now I am my own man, and nobody fucks with me. *(Pause.)*You can make of your body a vessel of strength. *(He does several quick push-ups, then rises, flushed and triumphant, flexing biceps.)* You can prepare for your day of release hoping it won't come too soon. *(Pause, as he rolls up his other sleeve, to reveal a tatto of a American eagle clutching a flag.)* Which is why they call me "Mister America"—NOBODY FUCKS WITH ME. *(A beat.)* *(Reflective, elegiac.)* eah—there was others. Never knew their names. Nor even faces. It's like the weather, the wind blowing the clouds across the Plains...never stops. *(Pause.)*

(PINKTOES may be addressing MR. AMERICA.)

PINKTOES. Wasn't ever identified—wasn't a "missing person." Momma kicked me out, I'm out. Took some of her money with me so I'm not missing, I'm out. Washed her of me... can't say I blame her.

MR. AMERICA. *(Matter-of-fact.)*Yeah I confessed—I guess. Told the Texas cops everything I could remember, all my fucking life—said "yes" to anything they asked me. Nine hours of it. Hell-bent for the electric chair I guess...

PINKTOES. NO! I'M TOO YOUNG TO DIE! *(Hides her face; pause.)* No.

HOMESICK

I accept my fate.

MR. AMERICA. *(Shrugs.)* Then the judge tossed it out—on account of I didn't have a lawyer. I told the cops I didn't want no fucking lawyer and I didn't—don't. O.K. but they talk so, they convince you. You need thr'py, he said. You're a casualty of our system. So, shit, O.K.—pleading guilty to "second-degree manslaughter" it was. I don't know. And all that past stuff I told the cops about the other girls—that's"delusion"— "con-fab-u-lation" they call it. *(Pause, bemused.)* Yeah, there's a deal with the court—seven-to-thirty years Up for parole in four years and I will be only forty-one then, not old. Not old, at all.

PINKTOES. They're thinking "Pinktoes" is from the Laredo stretch of I-35, or maybe east around Gainsville. Maybe one of the big cities—Houston, Dallas—where it's easy to get lost. Or maybe out of state. *(Pause, nodding.)* Yeah—one of them sad little shrinking towns in Kansas, Nebraska, Iowa nobody knows the name of except the folks who live there, and, for a while, till they forget, guys who pass through.

(Lights out.)

END OF PLAY

DR. MAGIC

DR. MAGIC was first performed at Bard College, New York, 2002.

CHARACTERS

DR. MAGIC: *Youthful middle age*
ALEX RINGER: *Mid thirties*
TRICIA RINGER: *Early or mid thirties*

(Lights up. DR. MAGIC stands before a mirror putting on stage makeup gray ing his hair with power. He whistles a tuneless tune of upbeat melancholy.)

DR. MAGIC. *(Addressing the audience, ordinary uninflated voice.)* One in each generation of my family has been so chosen: "Dr. Magic." It isn't a vocation. It isn't a "sacred calling." It isn't what you would call a career nor is it what you would call a curse, exactly. For us, it's what is. *(Affixing a mustache.)*

(Lights dim. We see DR. MAGIC putting on a tuxedolike jacket and preparing to stride forward stage front. Lights up. DR. MAGIC has become ebullient, genial, energized; smiling out into the audience. He is now in his stage personality, which might be described as restrained charisma. DR. MAGIC should not be played as parody)

DR. MAGIC. My name is Dr. Magic and I want to welcome you here this evening, ladies and gentlemen! Some of you are familiar faces, I see. *(Smiles at these.)* And many of you are new to the Land of Magic-welcome! I think I can safely predict that none of you will leave this hall quite the same as you entered it. *(Pause, peering into the audience.)* Now, who among those new to Dr. Magic will be my first volunteers of the evening?

(A beat. DR. MAGIC is both a seductive and an intimidating presence.)

DR. MAGIC. Ah, now: you-and you-have been on this stage before. I'm flattered of course but-shall we have someone who has never journeyed into the Land of Magic?

(MR. RINGER volunteers, impulsively. DR. MAGIC summons him to the stage.)

DR. MAGIC. And your companion, too, my friend! You would not wish to embark upon this journey without her.

(MR.and MRS. RINGER appear on stage beside DR. MAGIC. They are an at- tractive youngish couple, Well dressed and well groomed, slightly

DR. MAGIC

apprehensive; initially they are holding hands.)

DR. MAGIC. Welcome to the Land of Magic, my friends! You are a devoted married couple, I see.

MR. RINGER. It's our anniversary...

MRS. RINGER. *(Poking him; undertone.)* Oh, shhh!

DR. MAGIC. Your anniversary! Is it your-tenth? No-twelfth.

(The RINGERS profess astonishment that DR. MAGIC knows this fact.)

DR. MAGIC. *(With a modest bow.)* well, I am Dr. Magic, after all, Mr.and Mrs.-is it "Wrang"-"Wrangler"-

MR.RINGER."Ringer."

DR. MAGIC.*(Frowning with half-shut eyes.)* And your given name, son-something like-ex?-Tex?-no-

MRS. RINGER."Alea"!He's Alexander.

DR. MAGIC. And you are-Trixie?

MRS. RINGER."Tricia." Patricia.

(The RINGERS express awe at DR. MAGIC's powers. DR.. MAGIC behaves as if he has done nothing extraordinary.)

DR. MAGIC. It isn't a matter of "reading" minds, my friends, but only of hearing. For the air is aswarm with thoughts like musical notes-requiring a sympathetic ear.

MRS. RINGER. That's so...beautiful. I never heard anything like that before in my life.

DR. MAGIC. Thank you, Tricia. Now, tell me: have you two come here this evening on a journey of enlightenment, or mere curiosity? Or-merely to be entertained?

MR. RINGER. To celebrate our anniversary with something different-

MRS. RINGER. *(Overlapping.)* Enlightenment! Both of us.

DR. MAGIC. Please tell our audience where you hail from. Tricia and Alex.

MR. RINGER. Parsippany-

MRS. RINGER. -New Jersey.

DR. MAGIC. I knew it could't be "parsnips"-the word I was hearing. *(Pause.)* And what do you do in Parsippany, New Jersey, Alex?

MR. RINGER. I'm a junior vice president in sales and PR at Meckler Boxboard.

MRS. RINGER. The company has been downsizing, but Alex has been

DR. MAGIC

promoted.

MR. RINGER. I've been entrusted with, like, two jobs. An eighty hour week. Plus I kind of chauffeur Mr. Meckler's children after school. *(Quickly.)* I don't mind, though. "Double duty is trust"- that's a Meckler slogan.

MR. MAGIC. Congratulations, Alex. You sound like a young executive who won't be devoured in the feeding frenzy of our economic sea!

MR. RINGER. *(Blushing.)* I try, sir.

DR. MAGIC. And you, Tricia?

MRS. RINGER. *(Earnestly.)* Well, I try, too! I try very hard.

DR. MAGIC. At what do you try, Tricia? Tell us.

MRS. RINGER. To be a good person. A decent person. Every minute of my life, Dr. Magic, I try.

DR. MAGIC. A most unusual answer...from a most attractive young woman.

MRS. RINGER. I love my husband, Dr. Magic, and our two beautiful children, but I...oh, I seem to want more.

DR. MAGIC. More of what, my dear?

MRS. RINGER. Dr.Magic, I don't know. I came here tonight to be enlightened-by you.

MR. RINGER. *(Embarrassed.)* My wife gets spiritual sometimes, Dr. Magic.

MRS. RINGER. *(Intense.)* Since childhood I've awaited some sort of revelation, Dr. Magic. Oh, I'm religious; I'm a Christian; I'm "in love" and I've given birth, twice. What I await is something...of the soul. *(Pause.)* Sometimes I'm in terror that there really isn't anything more to me than this self, now. This. *(Glancing down at herself.)*

(A beat. DR. MAGIC appears distracted by MRS. RINGER.)

DR. MAGIC. *(Glancing at audience as if he has forgotten where he is.)* What? Oh, yes..."The Land of Magic." We must embark. *(Resuming his charismatic stage manner.)* Mr.and Mrs.Ringer, do you give your consent to be hypnotized this evening?

(The RINGERS nod with childlike shyness, anticipation.)

MR. RINGER. That's what we're here for...isn't it?

DR. MAGIC. That's a question you must answer yourselves. Are you?

(When the RINGER say yes DR. MAGIC swiftly waves his hand in front of their eyes. Almost immediately they begin to succumb.)

DR. MAGIC

DR. MAGIC. How heavy your eyelids are! Heavy as lead. How sleepy, how deliciously sleepy you are! Yet you can hear me clearly, Tricia and Alex, yes?

MR.,MRS. RINGER. Yes, Dr. Magic.

(They are in mild trances. Their eyes are nearly shut and their faces have gone slack.)

DR. MAGIC. When I snap my fingers, you will awaken-to a degree. When I wave my hand in this way *(He demonstrates.)* you will resume your trance. When I wave my hand in this way *(He demonstrates a more complicated gesture.)* You will lapse into a deeper trance from which only Dr. Magic can awaken you.

(The RINGER lapse into this deep trance. rigid as mannequins. DR. MAGIC genially addresses the audience as he sets out his props.)

DR. MAGIC. Hypnosis, ladies and gentleman, you will think is as old as mankind. In fact, it is older. Our primate ancestors are susceptible to falling into hypnotic trances under the right conditions. And more primitive animal and bird species are sometimes "hypnotized" as well. *(Pause.)* Usually it is predators who hypnotize their prey. As a kindness before devouring them.

(DR. MAGIC has taken up a hat pin. Shows its sharp point to the audience.)

DR. MAGIC. Sterilized, I guarantee! *(To the RINGERS.)* Alex and Tricia, this will tickle just a bit. Alex, you will sneeze, Tricia, you will blush. Neither of you will bleed.

(DR. MAGIC sticks MRS. RINGER's forearm with the pin. MR. RINGER giggles and sneezes. DR. MAGIC sticks MRS. RINGER 's forearm. MRS. RINGER giggles, and hides her face as if blushing. DR. MAGIC lifts the RINGER's arms for the audience to see.)

DR. MAGIC. You see? Not a drop of blood.

(DR. MAGIC abruptly sticks MR.and MRS.RINGER in their cheeks. They react as before.)

DR. MAGIC. *(To the audience, slyly.)* Not a drop of blood. *(Pause.)* "Mind

DR. MAGIC

over matter"-always. For matter is but mind, mastered.

(DR. MAGIC takes up a frayed top hat out of which he pulls a knee-length sock that he flutters in the air to show the audience.)

DR. MAGIC. *(Winking.)* The famously venomous king cobra of Malaysia. *(To MR. RINGER.)* Alex, when I snap my fingers you will awake, and you will see exactly what I have in my hand-a sock. You will accept it from me and exclaim in childlife delight, "Dr. Magic, thank you!" You will stand on your left leg, remove your right shoe, and put the stocking on your right foot. You will perform these actions spontaneously, without memory of my instruction. *(To MRS. RINGER, more intimately.)* Tricia. My dear. When I snap my fingers you will awake, and you will see in my hand a snake; the famously venomous king cobra of Malaysia.

(DR. MAGIC snaps his fingers. Both RINGERS awake groggily from their trances. They are somewhat disoriented as if they have been asleep for a long time. MRS. RINGER rubs her eyes seeing the stocking/snake in DR. MAGIC's hand.)

MRS. RINGER. *(Pulling at her husband's arm.)* Oh-oh-oh, Alex-oh-
MR. RINGER. *(Ignores her, seeing the stocking.)* Dr. Magic, thank you!

(As MRS. RINGER looks on in appalled disbelief, MR. RINGER takes the stocking from DR. MAGIC and performs the actions that DR. MAGIC has prescribed.)

MRS. RINGER. *(Panicked.)* Alex, no! No-
MR. RINGER. *(Lowered, embarrassed voice.)*Tricia, for God's sake! This is the opportunity of a lifetime.
MRS. RINGER. Alex! It will kill you!

(MR. RINGER struggles to clumsily pull the stocking onto his foot. MRS. RINGER backs away, emits breathless little sobs of terror.)

MR.RINGER. *(To MRS. RINGER.)* Darling, look what Dr. Magic has given me.
MRS. RINGER. Get away! Get away from me!
MR. RINGER. But, darling-aren't you happy for me?

DR. MAGIC

MRS. RINGER. I can't-I can't h-help you! Alex, get away from me!

MR. RINGER. A perfect fit! It was made for me. *(Walks about proudly.)*

DR. MAGIC. Now put your shoe back on, Alex. No need to lace up. You will wear home with you the first of Dr.Magic's gifts.

(MR. RINGER is boyishly pleased with the attention; MRS RINGER is nearly fainting.)

DR. MAGIC. *(To MRS. RINGER.)* My dear, a wife must grant to her husband a secret, passional life inaccessible to her. And respect it.

MRS. RINGER. But-he's crazy. That's snake he's w-wearing.

(DR. MAGIC snaps his fingers twice and both RINGERS awake more fully, unaware of what has happened. MRS. RINGER is puzzled and embarrassed that she has been perspiring, and surreptitiously wipes at her face with a tissue. MR. RINGER is embarrassed to see that one of his shoes is untied, and surreptitiously stoops to tie it.)

DR. MAGIC. Tricia and Alex Ringer of Parsippany, New Jersey: welcome to the Land of Magic. Are you ready to embark?

(The RINGERS rub their eyes. To them, no time has passed since they came on stage.)

DR. MAGIC. You've never been hypnotized before, eh?

(The RINGERS shake their heads, no.)

DR. MAGIC. Not even by Dr. Magic, eh?

(The RINGERS are puzzled by this question, but reply no.)

DR. MAGIC. We'll begin by asking you to sing for us, Tricia and Alex. A simple American tune-"White Christmas."

(The RINGERS are embarrassed, self-conscious.)

MR. RINGER. sing? Me? Hell, no.

MRS. RINGER. Oh, no! Not me.

DR. MAGIC. But Dr. Magic insists! Don't be shy.

DR. MAGIC

MRS. RINGER. I-I did sing in girl's chorus in high school. but I wasn't very good. My voice wavered on the high notes and sort of...hurt.

DR. MAGIC. No more stalling! Begin.

(The RINGERS, deeply embarrassed, make an effort. Their voices are weak.)

DR. MAGIC. Well, hmmm!-you've been out of practice a bit, Tricia. And you, Alex, you have a promising baritone voice in need of a few lessons. Let's see what Dr. Magic can do for you. *(He waves his hand to send the RINGERS into trances.)* Tricia and Alex, when I awaken you you will sing. And you will sing as I direct you, with passion, and some beauty.

(DR. MAGIC snaps his fingers to wake them.)

DR. MAGIC. "White Christmas, Tricia and Alex! Let's hear it.

(The RINGERS sing "White Christmas" with more assurance. Their voices waver initially, then become stronger as DR. MAGIC directs them, smiles, and praises them.)

DR. MAGIC. Well! Not bad, eh, ladies and gentlemen!

(The audience applauds. The RINGERS are confounded.)

MRS. RINGER. Oh, gosh...You don't need to...be nice...
MR. RINGER. You folks are...encouraging.
DR. MAGIC. Why did you think you couldn't sing?

(The RINGERS have no idea.)

DR. MAGIC. Individuals rarely know themselves, my friends. That's where Dr. Magic comes in. *(Waggishly.)* And how are your fitness quotients, Mr.and Mrs. Ringer from Parsippany?

(MR.and MRS. RINGER are uncertain what "fitness quotient" means. DR. MAGIC whistles loudly in emulation of a coach's whistle.)

DR. MAGIC. Seventh-grade gym! Rings, ropes, mats! Tricia, your nimble somersault.
MRS. RINGER. *(Frozen.)* Oh, I...can't.

DR. MAGIC

DR. MAGIC. Cartwheel!

MRS. RINGER. I c-can't, Dr. Magic. I'd break my neck.

DR. MAGIC. What about you, Alex? Can you still chin yourself fifty times? Do one hundred push-ups? Climb up a twenty-foot rope to the gym ceiling like a monkey, as you did whrn you were twelve?

MR. RINGER. Naw! No more.

DR. MAGIC. Hmmm.you are a bit overweight, Alex. Though you "work out"-"lift weights." *(Pinches flesh at MR. RINGER's waist.)* And you Tricia, tsk-tsk! *(Pats her hip.)*

MRS. RINGER. *(Mortified.)* I'm dieting all the time...almost.

DR. MAGIC. You need Dr. Magic's help, eh? *(DR.MAGIC waves his fingers and puts the RINGERS into trances.)*

(DR. MAGIC approaches the RINGERS individually.)

DR.MAGIC. *(To MR.RINGER.)* When I give this signal-(He shakes his fist.)-you will attempt to overpower the woman standing beside you. You will revert to an atavistic male self aroused and insatiable and you will slip behind the woman and slide your arm beneath her chin and attempt to throw her down, paying no heed to her cries for help. Yet your strength will be as water, and you will succumb to her power. *(To MRS. RINGER.)* When I give the signal-*(Shakes his fist.)*-you will step adroitly aside to elude your clumsy assailant, you will grab his wrist and fling him over your shoulder to the floor. You will be very strong, Tricia, because Dr. Magic's strength will flow through you, And you will not be afraid.

(DR. MAGIC lays a hand on MRS. RINGER's shoulder; his touch seems to course through her like an electric current. DR. MAGIC snaps his fingers to wake the RINGERS from their trances.)

DR. MAGIC. And so-Tricia and Alex Ringer-you're celebrating your twelfth wedding anniversary?

MR. RINGER. *(Slyly.)* Actually we've been together for, um-fourteen years.

MRS. RINGER. *(Embarrassed.)* Oh, Alex!

DR. MAGIC. Fourteen years, six months, nine days, eh?

(MR. and MRS. RINGER are speechless.)

DR. MAGIC

DR. MAGIC. *(Cupping his ear.)* Remember: Dr. Magic hears what you are thinking.

(DR. MAGIC shakes his fist. Like a sleepwalker, MR. RINGER attempts to attack MRS.RINGER. MRS.RINGER steps aside, seizes his wrist, and "flings" him over her shoulder to the floor. The action is clumsy but MR. RINGER winds up on the floor, dazed. Audience applauds, whistles. MRS.RINGER does an exuberant cartwheel. MR. RINGER cowers. DR. MAGIC helps him to his feet.)

MR. RINGER. What h-happened? Where am I? Is that woman my wife? Did she-attack me?
MRS. RINGER. *(Breathless, triumphant.)* No man will ever hurt me again. Bastards! See? See who I am? *(Flexes her arm muscles.)*
MR. RINGER. Tricia! My God.
DR. MAGIC. That's quite some woman, Alex! A real minx.
MR. RINGER. Dr.Magic, I I-love her. But I'm afraid of her.
DR. MAGIC. Go to sleep, son. You wounds will heal.

(DR. MAGIC puts MR. RINGER into a trance. MRS. RINGER, thrumming with energy, smiles suggestively at DR. MAGIC.)

DR. MAGIC. Tricia, that was remarkable. Your soul is emerging at last.
MRS. RINGER. I don't know what on earth came over me. Wow!
DR. MAGIC. Tell us what you feel, Tricia.
MRS. RINGER. I am feeling empowered. I am feeling as if dazzling lights have erupted in my brain and I will never, never die. I am feeling... *(Giggles.)*... sexy as hell. Like a man, I guess.

(Audience responds with applause, whistles.)

MRS. RINGER. Of course, I'm repentant, too. If I hurt him.
DR. MAGIC. Well, he did attack you, Tricia. You had no choice but to defend yourself.
MRS. RINGER. I had no choice... *(Laughs.)*
DR. MAGIC. Did you recognize your assailant?
MRS. RINGER. It was too dark.
DR. MAGIC. You won't press charges?
MRS. RINGER. The hell with "charges." This wild joy I can hardly contain...
(MRS. RINGER has been bouncing about the stage with girlish energy. She

is drawn to DR. MAGIC. She strokes his arm, lifts her face to be kissed. DR. MAGIC hesitates as if about to kiss MRS. RINGER. Instead, he waves his hand to put her to sleep.)

MRS. RINGER. *(Resisting.)* No! Not yet! Dr. Magic...

(DR. MAGIC waves his hand in the more complex way, to put MRS. RINGER into a deep trance. MRS. RINGER goes limp and slack as before. DR. MAGIC brushes her forehead with his lips.)

DR. MAGIC. I can't! Can't take advantage. It's in violation of the Hypnotists' Ethical Code.

(Change of lighting and mood. Ominous music.)

DR. MAGIC. *(To audience.)* With Dr. Magic in your head you are never alone.

(DR.MAGIC brings out stools and "electrical" props. These include wires, a switchboard and switch, electrodes. The Zapper may be simple or complicated as preferred. It may make a zapping noise when the switch is thrown.)

DR. MAGIC. *(Holding The Zapper aloft.)* The Zapper, ladies and gentlemen. Its terrible reputation precedes it. *(Pause.)* Of course it's just a magician's prop like any other; no source of electricity. It isn't plugged in and even if it were...*(He affixes and electrode to his arm and pulls the switch.)*... nothing happens.

(DR. MAGIC removes the electrode. He lays his hand on MR. RINGER's shoulder.)

DR. MAGIC. *(Paternal, kindly voice.)* When I awaken you from your little nap, Alex, you will obey me without hesitation. When I say the word "zap" you will zap-and zap-and zap. *(Snaps fingers.)*

(MR. RINGER wakes groggily from his trance. He is dazed, baffled by his disheveled, aching state. Hastily adjusts his clothing.)

DR.MAGIC. You do know where you are, Alex?

DR. MAGIC

MR.RINGER. Uh-I think so.

DR.MAGIC. You know who I am?

MR.RINGER. Oh, yes: you are Dr.Magic.

DR.MAGIC. Dr.Magic, your friend.

MR.RINGER. Dr.Magic, my friend.

DR.MAGIC. And you and Mrs.Ringer have come to me voluntarily, yes?

MR.RINGER. I-think so.

(MR.RINGER turns to MRS.RINGER who remains in her trance. MR.RINGER winces with pain.)

DR.MAGIC. Why, Alex, is something wrong?

MR.RINGER. Ow!*(Prevents one of his knees from buckling.)* Oh no, Dr. Magic, I'm fine.

DR.MAGIC. Not arthritic, are you, son? At your young age?

MR.RINGER. *(Quickly.)* No!

DR.MAGIC. You do appear a bit banged-up

MR.RINGER. From working out at the health club. Lifting weights, sit-ups...I do a little sparring.

DR.MAGIC. Yery good, Alex. You seem very fit to me. And I have some good news for you. *(Pause.)* You see here The Zapper.

MR.RINGER. Zapper...?

DR.MAGIC. You, Alex Ringer, have been selected to participate in a groundbreaking scientific experiment.

MR.RINGER. Me? Gosh.

DR.MAGIC. The sole junior executive at Meckle Boxboard to be so honored.

MR.RINGER.Gosh.

DR.MAGIC. Do you accept the challenge?

MR.RINGER. I sure do, Dr. Magic.

DR.MAGIC. The Zapper is an experiment to measure moral strength and stamina. The backbone of America. *(Pause.)*There are three participants required: the enforcer, the subject, and the coordinator. I am the coordinator, son, and you are the enforcer.

MR.RINGER. "Enforcer..." I like the sound of that.

DR.MAGIC. Your wife is the subject. You will be required to "zap" her with a mild electric current at appropriate intervals, as a test of her, and your, integrity.

MR. RINGER. Integrity...

DR. MAGIC. The Zapper is a fail-safe device, see? On a scale of one to ten, The Zapper's voltage is usually at one. Hardly more than a tickle, as you will see. Let's demonstrate. *(DR. MAGIC affixes the electrode to MR. RINGER.)* Now, I will pull the switch-

(MR. RINGER tenses.)

    DR. MAGIC. I told you, Alex: the shock is very mild. Hardly more than a tickle.
    MR. RINGER. *(Fearful, joking.)* I won't be electrocuted, will I?
    DR. MAGIC. Son, this nervousness isn't you. I'm disappointed.
    MR. RINGER. I'm sorry, sir! I'm not myself tonight, I feel sort of.. banged-up. My head...
    DR. MAGIC. Maybe Mrs.Ringer should be the enforcer, and you the subject.
    MR. RINGER. *(Quickly.)* Oh, no! Please throw the switch, Dr. Magic.

(DR. MAGIC throws the switch. MR. RINGER, very tense, reacts as if he has been mildly shocked. He sneezes.)

    DR. MAGIC. No need to sneeze this time, Alex. We'll try again.

(DR. MAGIC repeats the "zap" and this time MR. RINGER reacts with stoic fortitude.)

    DR. MAGIC. What'd I say? Hardly more than a tickle.
    MR. RINGER. Right! *(Wiping his forehead with a tissue.)*
    DR. MAGIC. It didn't hurt, Alex, did it?
    MR. RINGER. No...

(DR. MAGIC removes the electrode, and MR. RINGER rubs the "zapped" spot.)

    DR. MAGIC. The Zapper did not hurt you, and it will not hurt your wife. You will be increasing the voltage during the experiment but only in small increments. And only at my instruction.
    MR. RINGER. Yes, sir.
    DR. MAGIC. Aren't you going to ask what the experiment tests?
    MR. RINGER. Uh-integrity?
    DR. MAGIC. In more clinical terms the experiment is designed to measure "conditioned immunity." As the mild-very mild-voltage is made to increase by

the enforcer, the subject becomes immune to it until, with the final zap, the normal subject feels no more voltage than she felt at the outset. *(Pause.)* Of course, the subject is also being examined on her integrity.

MR. RINGER. My wife is a woman of integrity, Dr.Magic...If she isn't in one of her moods.

DR. MAGIC. There is no place in a scientific experiment for "moods." Remember, Alex, you too are being tested for moral strength: can you, will you, continue following directions even if your wife begins to imagine that she is feeling pain? For, of course, as I've demonstrated, there is no pain in this experiment.

MR. RINGER. "No pain in this experiment..."

DR. MAGIC. The Zapper is a harmless device, a kind of placebo.

MR. RINGER. "Placebo..." A test to see if the subject is...lying?

DR. MAGIC. We don't say "lying," Alex. The clinical term is "malingering." Or, in psychopathological terms, "confabulating."

MR. RINGER. *(Firmly.)* Lying by any other name is still lying.

(DR.MAGIC leads the hypnotized MRS.RINGER to a stool and seats her. Though not awake, MRS.RINGER seems aware of DR.MAGIC and turns her face yearningly toward him as toward the sun. Her movements are both childlike and seductive. DR.MAGIC affixes the electrode to MRS. RINGER's arm.)

DR. MAGIC. *(Soothing voice.)* Tricia!This is Dr. Magic! When I wake you, dear, your limbs will be heavy as lead; you will sit here unmoving as a pillar of cement. You have my permission to speak though. You can protest-if you feel you must. If you feel you are being mistreated.

(DR. MAGIC snaps his fingers to wake MRS. RINGER. She is groggy and dazed and glances about with wide, alarmed eyes.)

MRS. RINGER. Oh! Where am...*(Tries to move but cannot.)*

DR. MAGIC. *(Soothing, touching her shoulder.)* My dear, don't be alarmed. You know me, Dr. Magic.

MRS. RINGER. Yes, but...these other people...*(Blinks at MR. RINGER, who has been examining The Zapper with boyish excitement.)* Is that...Alex?

MR. RINGER. Honey, it's fine! We're fine. It's our anniversary, remember? We're in the Land of Dr. Magic.

MRS. RINGER. I...don't feel well. I want to go home.

MR. RINGER. You wanted to come here, Tricia. Dr. Magic was your idea.

DR. MAGIC

MRS. RINGER. *(Seeing electrode, wire.)* What's this?

MR. RINGER. We're doing an experiment together. It's fun.

DR. MAGIC. *(Kindly.)* Tricia, if you really want to go home so abruptly, if you want to abort this groundbreaking scientific experiment before we've even begun and sabotage Alex's opportunity to bring prestige to Meckler Boxboard, of course you are free to do so. That is a woman's prerogative.

(MRS.RINGER attempts to rise but cannot.)

MRS. RINGER. I...feel so heavy. So...guilty. *(With difficulty she manages to raise a hand to touch her forehead.)* Oh God, I must have done something... wicked.

DR. MAGIC. Well, you can make amends. You have only to cooperate with your husband and me. You will be rewarded; and then you can go home happy.

MRS. RINGER. I had a terrible dream that I...hurt...a loved one. And did a cartwheel over his body...Oh, God.

DR. MAGIC. Dreams, memories, moods-these have no place in scientific research, Tricia. *(Pause.)* You know of The Zapper, I think? You've overheard my instructions to your husband and so you know that The Zapper cannot hurt?

MRS. RINGER. "The Zapper cannot hurt..."

DR. MAGIC. This experiment is a simple one. I will ask you a question, and if you answer it truthfully, you will receive a point, if you fail to answer it truthfully, you will receive a zap.

MRS. RINGER. "...fail to answer it...receive a zap..."

DR. MAGIC. No zap will actually hurt, Tricia. No subject has ever been knocked into convulsions, nor even into unconsiousness. That is a fact.

MRS. RINGER. "Hurt...convulsions...fact."

DR. MAGIC. We'll demonstrate. A zap at one. *(About to instruct MR. RINGER to pull the switch as MRS.RINGER tenses.)* Alex-

MRS. RINGER. Oh! no...

MR. RINGER. *(Impatient.)* Honey, it's nothing. Hardly more than a tickle.

MRS. RINGER. I'm afraid.

MR. RINGER. I wasn't afraid. Don't be silly and ruin everything.

DR. MAGIC. It really is hardly more than a tickle, Tricia. Don't you want to try? For Dr.Magic?

MRS. RINGER. *(A wan smile.)* "For Dr. Magic." All right.

DR. MAGIC. Zap her, Alex.

DR. MAGIC

(MR.RINGER throws the switch.)

MRS. RINGER. Oh!
DR. MAGIC. *(Chiding.)* Now, Tricia, that didn't hurt, did it? Tell the truth.
MRS. RINGER. I...guess not.

(MR. RINGER nods eagerly, MRS. RINGER wanly.)

DR. MAGIC. Tricia, dear, we'll begin with a simple question. Who do you love best in all the world?
MRS. RINGER. Who do I l-love best...?
DR. MAGIC. Who in all the world?
MRS. RINGER. I guess...I'd have to choose...*(Pause, becoming agitated.)* Well, I'm a, a wife and a mother, and a d-daughter, I...
DR. MAGIC. *(Kindly.)* You must answer by the time I count five, Tricia. Or Alex will zap you. *(Begins counting "One...two...")*
MRS.RINGER. *(Overlapping, pleading.)* But, Dr. Magic, I...love them all... my f-family...my babies and...Alex and...oh, gosh...Mom and-
DR. MAGIC. Five! Zap her, Alex.

(MR. RINGER throws the switch.)

MRS. RINGER. Oh!
MR. RINGER. *(Undertone.)* That did not hurt.
MRS. RINGER. I l-love my husband, I...guess. Dr.Magic?
DR. MAGIC. It's too late for that question, dear. We'll move on
MRS. RINGER. I love Alex best. I do!

(MR.RINGER is hurt, offended; but does not deign to reply.)

DR. MAGIC. Was Alex your "first," Tricia?
MRS. RINGER. My "first"...what?
DR. MAGIC. Your first true love.
MRS. RINGER. *(Quickly.)* My f-first abiding love...The only man I ever wished to have babies with...
DR. MAGIC. Your first true love, Tricia. I think you know the distinction.
MRS. RINGER. I...Idon't know the distinction.
DR. MAGIC. Zap her, Alex. At two.
MR. RINGER. With pleasure! *(Throws the switch.)*
MRS. RINGER. Oh! That stung.

DR. MAGIC

DR. MAGIC. This question is a little trickier, dear. What is the capital city of Alaska?

MRS. RINGER. Anchorage-no, Fairbanks-Juneau?

DR. MAGIC. It's Juneau. Shall we allow that, Alex?

(MR. RINGER shrugs sullenly.)

DR. MAGIC. We'll give you a point, dear. Very good.

MRS. RINGER. *(Grateful to be praised.)* I remember from school. Alaska is one of the tricky ones.

DR. MAGIC. Now, dear: when did the War of 1812 begin?

MRS. RINGER. 1812?

DR. MAGIC. A point for you, dear! Very good. And when did the War of 1812 end?

(A beat.)

MRS. RINGER. Oh, I bet this is a trick...1812?

DR. MAGIC. Zap her, Alex. We'll stay at two.

(MR. RINGER throws the switch.)

MRS. RINGER. Oh!

DR. MAGIC. The War of 1812 ended, in a blaze of military glory, in 1815. How could any American high school graduate not remember?

MRS. RINGER. I'm so ashamed...

DR. MAGIC. Let's expand our boundaries, Tricia. What is the native name for Peking?

MRS. RINGER. Beijing?

DR. MAGIC. A point! Very good. And what is the native name for Rome?

MRS. RINGER. Roma!

DR. MAGIC. Very good. Another point.-Vienna?

(A beat.)

MRS. RINGER. *(Wild guess.)* W-Wein?

DR. MAGIC. *(Not expecting this.)* Ah, yes. "Wien." A tricky one which you got, dear. And-um-what is the native name for Berlin?

(A beat. MRS. RINGER shakes her head, baffled.)

DR. MAGIC

MRS. RINGER. Something like..."Verlin"?

DR. MAGIC. Zap her, Alex. At three.

MRS. RINGER. *(Registering surprise, pain.)* Oh! Alex, that hurts.

DR. MAGIC. Let's return to the personal sphere, Mrs. Ringer. If a unnamed party was your "first true love," was that party also your first sexual partner?

(A beat.)

DR. MAGIC. Or was Alex Ringer your first sexual partner?

(A beat.)

MRS. RINGER. Dr. Magic, I...don't need to answer that, do I? With all these people watching...

DR. MAGIC. Zap her, Alex. At four.

(MR. RINGER pulls the switch.)

MRS. RINGER. Oh, that hurts. Oh, Alex...

MR. RINGER. *(Undertone.)* Don't "Oh, Alex" me. You're vicious.

DR. MAGIC. We will escalate our experiment to voltage seven with the next question. What are Thomas Aquinas's five proofs of God's existence?

(MRS. RINGER is terrified.)

MRS. RINGER. Oh oh oh...Alex, don't! Alex, please...don't zap me...

DR. MAGIC. That isn't your answer, Tricia, is it? I'll count to five. One... two...*(Continues count.)*

MRS. RINGER. *(Overlapping.)* Alex, no! Oh, Alex, it hurts...

MR. RINGER. *(Undertone.)* It does not hurt.

DR. MAGIC. Five! Alex, zap her.

(A beat. MR. RINGER hesitates.)

DR. MAGIC. What are you waiting for, Alex? Dr. Magic says zap her.

(MR. RINGER pulls the switch. MRS. RINGER screams.)

DR. MAGIC. We have no choice but to escalate to eight. The subject has

DR. MAGIC

racked up only four points. Mrs. Ringer-

MRS. RINGER. *(Quivering.)* No! Don't! I'm sorry for being vicious! I'll never behave like a man again. Alex, forgive me!

(MR. RINGER maintains a stony composure.)

MRS. RINGER. You know that I love you, Alex. My life would have no meaning with you. *(Distraught.)* I mean-without you.

DR. MAGIC. Since theology is obviously not your strength, Tricia, let's try science. Is the Earth forty-five million years old, four hundred and fifty million years old, or 4.5 billion years old?

(A beat.)

MRS. RINGER. *(Cringing, almost a whisper.)* It's a trick, isn't it? It'sn-none of those?

DR. MAGIC. Is that your answer, Tricia?

MRS. RINGER. No! Wait-

DR. MAGIC. Give an educated guess, dear. The enforcer is getting impatient over there.

MRS. RINGER. *(Pleading.)* But I'm not educated. I graduated from college but-oh, God, I don't seem to know anything.

DR. MAGIC. Zap her, Alex. The subject is clearly obfuscating.

(A beat.)

DR. MAGIC. Alex! Zap her. Dr. Magic has spoken.

MR. RINGER. I...I can't seem to, Dr. Magic. *(Drops The Zapper onto the floor.)*

DR. MAGIC. Pick that up, Mr. Ringer. Immediately.

(MR. RINGER kicks The Zapper away from him.)

DR. MAGIC. Are you sabotaging the experiment, Alex? Sabotaging your own career?

MR. RINGER. *(Stony, stricken.)* I...I can't hurt her.

DR. MAGIC. *(Furious.)* I've told you, The Zapper does not hurt. I command you to pick it back up, and continue.

(MR. and MRS. RINGER remain in their places as if paralyzed. DR. MAGIC

DR. MAGIC

waves his hand to put them both into deep trances.)

DR. MAGIC. Insubordination! I sentence you to the deepest depths of your empty heads and may you never waken!

(DR.MAGIC suddenly remembers that the audience is present. He attempts a more genial manner.)

DR. MAGIC. Ladies and gentlemen! Nothing like this has ever happened to Dr.Magic brfore, I assure you. It will never happen again, I promise.

(DR. MAGIC circles the RINGERS who, in their comatose state, are nonethe -less holding hands.)

DR. MAGIC. *(Relenting.)* Oh, all right. *(Removes the electrode from MRS. RINGER's arm.)* Tricia and Alex, when I wake you from your deep trance, you will remember nothing of this evening except: it has been the happiest evening of your life. You will love each other through your natural lives and you will recall-dimly, as in a dream-"Dr. Magic" with love, too. This is your gift from Dr. Magic.

(DR. MAGIC snaps his fingers and backs away into the shadowns. Exits. Lights on the RINGERS, who wake slowly and with difficulty from their trances as the rest of the stage darkens. The RINGERS clutch at each other in silence.)

(Lights out.)

END OF PLAY

HERE SHE IS!

HERE SHE IS was first performed at the Philadelphia Festival Theatre for New Plays, 1995.

CAST

BARBARA: *44*
MISS ALABAMA: *Early 20's; secretly a transvestite*
MISS ALASKA: *Early 20's; black*
MISS NEW YORK: *Early 20's*
LIZ: *Any age over 30*
M.C.: *Middle-aged or older*
STAGEHAND 1: *Young man*
STAGEHAND 2: *Young man*

(LIGHTS UP. An empty stage with a brief runway. Isolated props. An American flag on a tacky "gold" pedestal, of a kind seen in public school auditoriums. BARBARA enters slowly, glancing about in perplexity. She is a suburban woman in the city for the day; her glasses are of a slightly outmoded "stylish" style; She is neatly groomed, moderately attractive, very conventionally dressed; carrying a "good" purse and several packages, predominantly a Bloomingdale's shopping bag. Enter, crossing BARBARA's path without noticing her, deep in conversation, MISS ALABAMA, MISS ALASKA, and MISS MICHIGAN. The three young women are strikingly attractive, and heavily made up; they wear skin-tight jeans, high-heeled shoes, and showy designer blouses or sweaters; their long nails are polished, their hair dramatic and eye-catching, their jewelry a bit excessive. Their voices are stagey melodic murmurs.)

MISS ALABAMA. *(Southern accent)* I declare, I'm scared stiff! You girls all know this part of the country but I never been so far north before!

MISS ALASKA. *(Holding out her shaky, but very pretty hands)* I've never been so far south before! I'm scared petrified!

MISS MICHIGAN. *(Cooing "black" cadences)*Ohhh man, what about me? Who's goin to look at me for myself? I'm a walking talkin in-yo'-face political statement!

(Enter MISS NEW YORK, as the three young women are about to exit. MISS NEW YORK, with extravagant long ripply russet-red hair, and a "statuesque" body, is the most glamorous of all. She trips along fetchingly in her high-heeled pumps.)

MISS NEW YORK. Oooohhh! guys!—wait for me! You going to rehearse your routines?

MISS ALABAMA. Nah, we're going up the block to the I CAN'T BE-LIEVE IT'S YOGURT. C'mon!

(BARBARA has been staring at the young women in amazement.)

HERE SHE IS!

BARBARA. *(Calling out belatedly after them.)* Excuse me—?

(MISS NEW YORK, MISS ALABAMA, MISS ALASKA, and MISS MICHGAN exit, arms around one another's waists, giggling happily. LIZ, the production manager, enters briskly, having sighted BARBARA. She is a practical-minded woman of any age beyond 30.)

LIZ. *(Vexed, relieved.)* Oh, there you are, Miss Utah! We've been looking all over for you.

BARBARA. For me?

LIZ. *(Displaying wristwatch.)* Isn't it 5:25, Miss Utah?

BARBARA. It is, But...

LIZ. Where's your production schedule, Miss Utah? Your rehearsal was to begin promptly at 5:15.

BARBARA. Why do you call me "Miss Utah"? My name is—

LIZ. *(Impatiently.)* We don't have time for names here, Miss Utah. Names come and go every season; states abide forever. We're on the air in two and a half hours. *(Staring.)* Is that your dance costume?

BARBARA. Dance costume?

LIZ *(Snapping fingers, yelling.):* Music up, Jerry! Check out the sound system.

(Brisk syncopated music for tap dancing comes on; perhaps a wildly syndicated version of "Tea For Two.")

BARBARA. I'm afraid there's been a—misunderstanding? I'm from Katonah, not Utah. I have no connection with Utah. I'm in the city just for today, exchanging some of my daughter's birthday presents, and right now I'm looking for apartment #13D, the name is Cottler—?

(LIZ, who hasn't been listening, takes the Bloomingdale's bag from BARBARA, removes a modish sexy-punky costume. Perhaps a leather mini-skirt, or a black cat-suit. The latest in ephemeral teen fashion.)

LIZ. O.K., Miss Utah, quick-change. We're behind schedule and the boss will be furious if he finds out.

BARBARA: Excuse me—what? C-Change? *(As LIZ thrusts the clothes at her)* Here?

LIZ. Honey, you don't want to face our live audience and one hundred million TV viewers raw and unrehearsed, do you? Think of the good folks

HERE SHE IS!

back in Utah, pinning their hopes on you.

BARBARA. *(Unaccountably changing her clothes, with desperate swiftness, even as she protests.)*B-But I'm not from Utah, I'm from Katonah, New York! I took the Amtrak in this morning and I'm scheduled to take it back at seven! I thought this was the Atlantic Apartments, 668 West End Avenue?— but where is 13D?— my old Bryn Mawr roommate is expecting me—

LIZ . *(Yelling.)* Louder, Jerry!

(Music louder.)

BARBARA. —and my husband is expecting me home in time to make dinner. He'll be terribly upset if—

LIZ. *(Helping BARBARA with costume.)*Wow! This is chic.

BARBARA. But—it's Terrill's, a size 6, isn't it a little too— snug—on me?

LIZ. Honey, in our pageant, skin isn't too snug. *(Snapping fingers.)* O.K.—one time through.

BARBARA. Isn't this the Atlantic Apartments, 668 West End Avenue? Did I step into the wrong building?

LIZ. *(About to remove BARBARA's glasses.)*We'll just take these off.

BARBARA. *(Resisting firmly.)* Oh, no: I always wear my glasses. They hide the bags under my eyes.

(BARBARA begins to tap dance. Hesitant at first; then inspired; surprisingly good. During her brief performance of a minute or two, MISS ALABAMA, MISS ALASKA, MISS MICHIGAN, and MISS NEW YORK enter to watch. They are eating yogurt cones or sundaes and rapidly lose their appetites.)

MISS ALABAMA. Ohhh my Gawd—which one of us is that?

MISS ALASKA. Talk about natural talent—wow!

MISS NEW YORK. That's Miss Utah!—ohhh that smooth skin! those teeth! eyes! hair! Glowing with health!

MISS MICHIGAN. —The "natural" look—oh, man!

MISS ALABAMA. Miss Utah makes me feel kinda, ohh kinda—synthetic?

MISS ALASKA. She makes me feel I better go back and floss my teeth one more time—

MISS NEW YORK. I better shampoo my hair one more time—

MISS MICHIGAN. I better do my nails one more time—

MISS ALABAMA. I better rethink my strategy one more time—

HERE SHE IS!

(MISS ALABAMA, MISS ALASKA, MISS MICHIGAN, MISS NEW YORK shrink away, exit. The music has been cut off rudely. BARBARA continues dancing for a beat or two before she realizes.)

LIZ. *(Sincerely applauding.)*Miss Utah, that's terrific! Since our pageant was inaugurated in 1921, I've never seen a performance so—heartfelt.

BARBARA. *(Suddenly anxious.)*Was I—all right? I'm sort of—out of—practice— *(She is breathless, adjusting glasses, hair, costume, pantyhose.)*

LIZ. I mean—terrific! You'll win the judges' hearts, I just know.

BARBARA. I w-will? The judges' hearts?

LIZ. *(Looking through BARBARA's other shopping bags)*Where's your evening attire?

BARBARA. Evening attire?

LIZ. Never mind, we've got some extras—left over from previous competitions. *(Exiting, yelling.)* Maggie—?

(LIGHTS UP on the M.C. He is a puffy middle-aged man in a tuxedo with a red satin cummerbund; there is orangish pancake makeup on his face and he wears an obvious toupee. Enters frowning at himself in a pocket mirror; wets and smooths eyebrows, practices puckers and smiles.)

BARBARA. Excuse me, sir—

M.C.. *(Big glistening smile.)* Ah, hah: Miss—is it Nevada? No! *(Snaps fingers.)* Colorado?—no! *(Snaps fingers.)* Wyoming?—no!

BARBARA. Utah?

M.C.. Utah!—of course. Great ol' state.

BARBARA: But I'm not from Utah.

M.C.. *(Chuckling.)*That's what we all say, when we have stage fright. *(Mimicry of female terror.)* "I'm not from Utah!"

BARBARA. I think there's been some confusion—

M.C.. *(Immediate reaction.)*What? Confusion? Where? Whose? *(Vehemently.)* Everything is going smoooothly and professsionally exactly as it has since our first competition in 1921.

BARBARA. Competition?

M.C.. Well, we don't like to stress that, Miss Utah. "Pageant" sounds a whole lot better—kinder.

BARBARA. But I am not from Utah! You're mistaking me for someone else! I was born in Greenwich, Connecticut—I live in Katonah, New York with my husband and two children—I'm in the city just for today—and at the moment I'm looking for apartment 13D?—I'm sure I stepped into the right

building—
    M.C.. Hmmm! Which building?
    BARBARA. The Atlantic Apartments at 668 West End Avenue—
    M.C.. This is Atlantic City.

(A beat.)

    BARBARA. W-What?
    M.C.. *(A hearty chuckle.)* It's just stage fright, Miss Utah. I know the symptoms. *(He checks her pulse.)* Rapid pulse— *(Touches her forehead.)* Feverish skin plus cold clamminess— *(Squeezes her hands.)* Nerves! You gals are the creme de la creme of American womanhood—beauty, brains, sweetness, goodness—but out on that runway it's dog-eat-dog, eh?—or do I mean cat-eat-cat?—only one of you will wear a crown tonight. Hell, I'm nervous myself— *(Displays his badly shaking hands, smiling broadly.)* —even an old show biz pro like me.
    BARBARA. How did I get in Atlantic City? I took a cab from Bloomingdale's to 668 West End Avenue—I stepped into the foyer of the Atlantic Apartments—
    M.C.. You got here, honey, because you're a winner. You already beat out millions of rivals and tonight—if you're lucky—you'll beat out fifty-one more. "creme de la creme"—see?

(M.C. walks off, taking out his pocket mirror to check his hair. BARBARA
    stares after him.)

    BARBARA. Oh my God! That man is—Bert Reynolds? My mother's old heart throb? It can't be—can it?

(LIZ reappears.)

    LIZ. Miss Utah! Come on!
    BARBARA. Wh-what? Where?

(LIZ marches BARBARA offstage.)

    LIZ. All you states have to be lined up!

(LIGHTS UP on MISS ALABAMA and MISS ALASKA in glamorous low-cut
    evening gowns. Staring critically at themselves in a full-length mirror.)

HERE SHE IS!

MISS ALABAMA. That Miss Utah!—she's got guts.

MISS ALASKA: Makes me wince seeing myself now. "Miss Alaska"— huh!

MISS ALABAMA. I was so damn proud being "Miss Alabama"—now, I declare I just don't know. *(Shoring up her sizable bosom in both hands.)* In the presence of a natural woman—

MISS ALASKA. *(Adjusting a false eyelash.)*—unadorned beauty—

MISS ALABAMA. —sincerity—

MISS ALASKA. —maturity—

MISS ALABAMA. —plus talent, brains—

MISS ALASKA. —true femininity—

MISS ALABAMA. You want to cry out and declare your own true self, don't you?

MISS ALASKA. *(Grimly.)*If you have the guts.

(LIGHTS DOWN ON MISS ALABAMA, MISS ALASKA. LIGHTS UP ON MISS MICHIGAN. In an equally glamorous evening gown, putting on the final touches of lipstick, powder; brooding into a mirror.)

MISS MICHIGAN. Well, girl!—are you proud of yourself for scrambling to the top of the meretricious white bourgeoise slave market?— or are you just plain ashamed? "Miss Michigan"—huh!

(LIGHTS DOWN ON MISS MICHIGAN. LIGHTS UP ON MISS NEW YORK. In her evening gown, similarly primping and brooding into a mirror.)

MISS NEW YORK. "Miss New York"!—tinsel in the mouth, now you're made to see your hypocrisy—duplicity—mendacity—falsity—set beside a true, brave woman. Aren't you ashamed! From nursery school through junior high-from junior high to this very moment—you've played a role in others' eyes—mainly men—your inner worth reflected in their vision, and not your own. *(Lifts her long ripply hair, lets fall in a cascade.)* Ah, "Miss New York"!— if you had the guts.

(LIGHTS DOWN ON MISS NEW YORK. LIGHTS TO DIM. LIZ runs across the stage.)

LIZ. The call is five minutes. Three minutes. Two minutes. Everybody ready!

HERE SHE IS!

(A curtain closes on the stage. LIGHTS OUT. Music: "Here She Is, Miss America" sung by a male vocalist, with unembarrassed passion. LIGHTS UP on the curtain as it opens to reveal M.C., striding forward, singing, arms uplifted to the audience. Thunderous taped applause.)

M.C.. Thank you, thank you, ladies and gentlemen! *(Broadly smiling, blowing kisses.)*Thank you!

(More applause.)

M.C.. Oh, you're a wonnnderfull audience!—some of you regulars have been with us since 1921!—God bless your warm, uplifting faces!

(M.C. wipes at his eyes. More applause.)

M.C.. Have we got a pageant for you tonight! Ladies and gentlemen, this year's crop of American beauties is the true creme de la creme!—the richest most spectacular harvest since our prestigious competition began. But first a word from our—

(Theme music comes up, but BARBARA, apparently misreading a cue, enters uncertainly, blinking and squinting in the light. A few scattered handclaps. BARBARA is wearing a pink taffeta prom dress, strapless; a shiny banner MISS UTAH is draped across her breasts. White gloves, rhinestone earrings. Glasses as before.)

M.C.. *(Rattled.)* B-But first—a word from our sponsor—?
BARBARA. *(Petrified with stage fright, wide-eyed.)*I—I'm supposed to introduce myself now? My name is, um, B-Barbara Utah— I mean Miss Utah, and I'm th-th-thrilled to be here tonigjht... *(Hyperventilating.)* My h-home state is New York but for s-some reason I'm honored to represent the great state of Utah at this Pageant—so, folks back in Utah, HI! *(Waving, a ghastly smile; then pause, sudden thought.)* Oh my God! I came out too soon, didn't I?
M.C.. *(Smoothing over blunder, clapping.)* Miss Utah!—welcome to Atlantic City, New Jersey! You're just in the nick of time, isn't she, folks?— this great-looking gal? Mmmmm, not a nanosecond too soon!

(M.C. leads enthusiastic applause.)

HERE SHE IS!

BARBARA. *(undertone to M.C.)* Sh-Should I go back? I forgot my cue—

(BARBARA tries to flee stage in panic; M.C. restrains her.)

M.C.. No, no, no, Miss Utah! As long as you are here— *(Broad wink at audience.)* —tell us a little about yourself.

BARBARA. W-What do you want to know? I'm from Katonah, New York, and—

M.C.. *(Cutting her off.)* I bet you sewed that fetching taffeta gown with your own two hands, Miss Utah, didn't you?

BARBARA. No.

M.C.. No?

BARBARA. *(Swallowing, deadly earnest.)*I haven't touched my Singer sewing machine for years. I don't even know where it is. That nice woman— *(A vague gesture toward the wings.)* —found this for me in a dressing room.

M.C.. Well, it's very, very pretty—

BARBARA. *(Awkwardly cutting him off.)*The funny thing is, it's exactly like my senior prom dress—I wore to my senior prom at Greenwich High— twenty-six years ago next June! *(Caressing the material.)* The identical shade of pink!

M.C.. Did you sew your senior prom gown, Miss Utah?

BARBARA. No. We bought it at Bloomingdale's, in the city.

M.C.. Well—it's a coincidence anyway, isn't it, folks? *(Leads brief applause, smiling broadly.)* A good luck omen, maybe?

BARBARA. Is it time for my tap dance now?

M.C.. *(Forced grin.)*The Talent Peformances are a little later in our program, Miss Utah. Right now, we'd like you to tell us about yourself.

(A beat. BARBARA stares and blinks.)

BARBARA. *(Awkward laugh.)* My mind just went—blank.

M.C.. *(A wink at audience)* How could you tell, Miss Utah?

(Loud (taped) laughter, a smattering of applause.)

BARBARA. I had something to say and—my mind just went blank.

M.C.. Hmmm, yes. Miss Utah, let's move to the General Questions part of the program. How can the United States most effectively pay off the national debt, combat crime and illiteracy, and remain the world's Number One protector of democracy? Fifteen seconds for your answer!

HERE SHE IS!

BARBARA. *(Adjusting her glasses, almost crossly.)* For God's sake, why ask me? What do I know? Don't we elect qualified people to public office so that, in turn, they can hire qualified advisors? Isn't that what our taxes are for?

(Loud applause.)

M.C.. *(Clapping too)* Right on, Miss Utah! You shoot from the hip.

BARBARA. All I have is a B.A. from Bryn Mawr, Class of '72. I majored in English, I don't know anything.

(Laughter, applause.)

BARBARA. Is it time for my tap dance now?

(Sudden tap dance music up. BARBARA begins to dance, with surprising energy and skill. M.C. is drawn into tap dancing with her briefly, as if they're old partners. Thunderous applause.)

M.C.. *(Wiping face with handkerchief.)* Wowee, Miss Utah! That was sure some fun!

(BARBARA bows. Tugging up her gown, which is slipping.)

M.C.. But—hmmm!—back to Broader Issues. Tell us, Miss Utah; Do you believe in Life Everlasting?

BARBARA. *(An unthinking expression of utter dismay.)* Oh, this couldn't go on and on forever—could it? *(Hand to mouth, wide-eyed.)* Ooops!

(Laughter, applause. Isolated cheers.)

BARBARA. *(Quickly.)* Of course, I believe in Life Everlasting. And in God the Father—or whatever He is: people are debating these days maybe He isn't male. Whatever—I believe.

(Applause comes up.)

BARBARA. *(Squinting out anxiously into audience.)* There is a purpose to all this—there's got to be. *(Almost pleading.)* Doesn't there?

M.C.. *(Leading audience in applause)* Words of sheer wisdom, Miss

HERE SHE IS!

Utah! Must be that western air, eh? So fresh, pure—now that nuclear testing is forbidden. *(Pause, salacious smile)* Tell us, Miss Utah—this is crucial—do you ride a horse?

BARBARA. A horse?

M.C.. *(Gesturing lewdly.)* HORSE. You're on top, he's on the bottom.

(Much laughter, applause.)

M.C.. *(Sniggering to audience.)* I see we have some HORSE LOVERS out there tonight!

BARBARA. Excuse me, I—I've been trying to explain for hours—I'm not from Utah.

M.C.. *(Chuckling.)* Folks, that's code for stage fright— "I'm not from Utah!" *(Wriggles hips, gives a female shriek.)* "OOOOHHH I'M NOT FROM UTAH"

BARBARA. *(Pleading.)* But I'm not. I wouldn't want anyone to think I'm here under false pretenses—I don't have any connection with Utah at all.

M.C.. *(Humoring her.)* No connection with Utah, Miss Utah?

BARBARA. No connection. *(Pause, hand to mouth.)* Ooops!

M.C. *(A wink at audience.)* What did you just remember, Miss Utah? Can you share it with our studio audience and one hundred million TV viewers?

BARBARA. *(Blushing, shakes head.)* I, um—n-no...

M.C.. *(Shaking forefinger, chiding.)* Now, Miss Utah! Prime time American TV is truth-telling time, you know that.

BARBARA. I, I—just can't say—I'm so embarrassed—

M.C.. Can't say—what?

BARBARA. I just remembered, I was— *(She leans to the M.C. to whisper in his ear.)*

M.C. . *(Loudly, gleefully.)* "—conceived in Dinosaur National Park, Utah, July 1950, on my parents' honeymoon"—! Wowee!

(Wild applause, laughter.)

(BARBARA tries to smile like a good sport; can't bear it, and hides her face. More laughter.)

M.C.. *(Leering, winking at audience.)* I'd say that was some connection, eh folks?

HERE SHE IS!

(More laughter. BARBARA peers through her fingers, guilty and childlike, as if into a TV camera.)

BARBARA. Mom?—Dad? Are you watching? Gee, I'm sorry if I embarrassed you!

M.C.. *(Leaning in, mugging.)* Mmmmm Mom?—Dad? I'd say you two honeymooners did pretty well. Congratulations! Must be that raunchy Dinosaur air, eh?

(BARBARA lets her hands fall from her face.)

BARBARA. *(Staring at M.C.)* Excuse me, sir—I've got to ask, for Mom's sake. Are you Bert Reynolds?

(M.C. continues playing to the audience, unhearing.)

BARBARA. You do look like Bert Reynolds...sort of. He was a big movie star of the 1950's, I guess...my mother's old heart throb. In those days, even married women had "heart throbs" and they weren't ashamed to admit it, they were encouraged. Except, Mr. Reynolds, I thought you were, um, deceased.

M.C.. *(Big smile.)* Reports of my demise are GREATLY EXAGGERATED, dear, And nowwwww—

(M.C. gestures broadly and music comes up, A luridly sweetened and syncopated version of "America the Beautiful.")

M.C.. Your cue, Miss Utah.
BARBARA: My cue—?
M.C.. Your cue, Miss Utah.
BARBARA. My cue—?
M.C.. *(Impatiently, overlapping.)* Let's see what Utah's got the rest of the states haven't!

(M.C. rather forcibly helps BARBARA strip off her gown. She is wearing a swim suit beneath. Her swim suit is prim and old-fashioned. BARBARA, stiff with terror, ventures out onto the runway. She tries to move with the bouncy music, but can't. She tries what she knows of a model's slinky glide, but can't. A turn, a pirouette, a ghastly smile; her glasses slide down her nose and her strapless suit is slipping. Music goes down for

HERE SHE IS!

BARBARA's epiphany.)

BARBARA. *(Peering at audience)*You...aren't really there, are you? And I'm not here, exactly...am I? This is a dream...isn't it? I'm a forty-four-year-old housewife and mother from Katonah competing in the Miss American Pageant at Atlantic City and it's all a wild, lurid dream...isn't it?

(Music shifts to "Here She Is, Miss America." M.C. sings with unabashed phony passion, gestures.)

M.C.. "Here she is—MISS UTAH! Here she is—OUR IDEAL!

BARBARA. *(More intense, engaging audience.)* Mom? This is your dream, not mine—is that it? Mom? You can wake up now, Mom— please.

(LIGHTS OUT on BARBARA. LIGHTS UP on MISS ALASKA. In her evening gown, a shiny banner MISS ALASKA across her breasts.)

MISS ALASKA. *(Winning smile, seductive, sweet.)* Thank you, ladies and gentlemen! I'm just so THRILLED to be here tonight to introduce myself! *(Pause)* When I was crowned Miss Alaska a few months ago, on the very eve of my mother's death, it was the happiest day of my life, I tell you. I was THRILLED and DELIGHTED and THRUST ALL PANGS OF CONSCIENCE behind me that Mom was dying of brain cancer in a charity ward in the bush beyond the Arctic Circle— *(Smiling sweetly.)* —I figured, what the heck, Mom was an alcoholic, too. *(Pause.)* What did I care?—I was fiercely pursuing my American dream of becoming, first, MISS ALASKA, and, second, MISS AMERICA— so that I could move out of Alaska as fast as possible, and pursue my career as a model, actress, party girl, top-level executive and maybe go for being the next Mrs. Trump. *(Pause.)* Does that surprise you? Why should it? There's more— *(She seductively places an "Eskimo" hood on her head, taking care not to displace her hair.)* I AM NOT A U.S. CITIZEN. Does that surprise you?

(Through MISS ALASKA's speech the audience has been restive; now we hear isolated boos and catcalls. MISS ALASKA strips provocatively to her glamorous swim suit.)

MISS ALASKA. That's right, folks: I lied. My life is a lie: I lie all the time: I LIKE TO LIE. I am not a citizen of your ridiculous country—I forged my birth certificate when I was eight years old, to get into school. My mother was

HERE SHE IS!

Inuit—the white- racist term for which is "Eskimo." My father is Canadian, and if I'm a citizen of any country it's Canada, where I was born in the Northwest Territory. *(Pause.)* Want to know more?—I've been letting my body hairs sprout these last few hours. See? *(Lifts arms to reveal underarm stubble; indicates stubble on legs.)*

(Outraged response from audience. LIGHTS OUT.)
(LIGHTS UP on MISS MICHIGAN, who is already in her swim suit, the shiny banner MISS MICHIGAN across her breasts. She strides out on the runway, very much in control; a sexy-jaunty swagger. Pauses on the runway, arms akimbo in a provocative pose.)

MISS MICHIGAN. *(Dazzling smile.)* Everything I said about myself is true—I'm a straight-A student at Michigan State where I'm studying pre-med 'cause I hope to practice family medicine, I'm captain of the women's swim team. I'm a member of the NAACP and a volunteer Red Cross worker and I'm active in an anti-drug program in East Lansing and I'm a vegetarian and I just love Jane Austen and Winston Marcellus—except—and here I did fib a little: I am not a Sunday School teacher, nor even a member of any church. *(Pause.)* Why?—'cause I DON'T BELIEVE IN GOD.

(Boos, catcalls.)

MISS MICHIGAN. *(Taking it all in with satisfaction.)* Right! This girl's a born FREE THINKER. Never could swallow that fairy tale shit of a BIG WHITE DADDY in the sky—or any DADDY at all.

(Growing angry repsonse.)

MISS MICHIGAN. *(Taunting.)* Uh-huh. There's more. Yo' looking at a RADICAL FEMINIST. *(Pause.)* There's more—yo' looking at a RADICAL LESBIAN FEMINIST. And these front teeth—*(Taps them.)* —are FALSE.

(LIGHTS OUT to outraged response. LIGHTS UP on MISS NEW YORK in her glamorous swim suit, a shiny banner MISS NEW YORK across her breasts. Her beautiful hair has been cut and styled as a mohawk and she wears earring clamps and a nose ring.)

MISS NEW YORK. *(Beaming.)* Plus I vomit thrice daily to gorge and keep my figure; and I'm actually not a "miss"—I've been married and divorced

HERE SHE IS!

three times.

(Boot, catcalls, whistles.)

    MISS NEW YORK. To the same woman!

(LIGHTS OUT on MISS NEW YORK.)
(LIGHTS UP on MISS ALABAMA, in her glamorous swim suit with a shiny
    banner MISS ALABAMA across her breasts, and the flush-faced M.C.
    who is trying to prevent her from striding along the runway. They tussel;
    M.C. loses his balance and sits down, hard; MISS ALABAMA strips off
    false eyelashes, false fingernails, her wig, and reveals that she is wear-
    ing a padded bra.)

    MISS ALABAMA. *(Man's voice)* I'm not a GIRL—I'm a GUY!

(Outraged response from audience. LIGHTS OUT STROBE LIGHTS. M.C.,
    LIZ, other unidentified figures run about in an emergency state. Cries,
    shouts of dismay and anger. LIGHTS OUT. In DARKNESS, theme music
    again, as if nothing has gone wrong. LIGHTS UP on BARBARA, still in
    her swim suit, being crowned Miss America with a phonily gleaming
    "gold" crown. Her shiny banner now reads MISS AMERICA. The dazed,
    disheveled, grim M.C. lowers the crown on her head as he sings.)

    M.C.. *(Flat, forced voice.)* "Here she is—MISS AMERICA! Here she
is—OUR IDEAL!
    BARBARA. *(Wiping at her eyes.)* Oh, thank you—oh, I can't believe
this—oh, it's a dream come true—
    M.C.. *(Waxing more passionate.)* "Here she is—MISS AMERRRICAAA!
Here she is—OUR IDEEALL!
    BARBARA. *(Waving at camera.)* Mom? Dad? Charles? Terrill? Ricky? HI!
SORRY I didn't get home to make dinner! *(Pause; a thought strikes her.)*
Ooops! I'm not qualified to be Miss America, either—I'm a "Mrs.", not a
"Miss."

(Boos, catcalls, hisses and instantaneous LIGHTS OUT. LIGHTS UP. Empty
    stage, as at the start. A beat or two. STAGEHAND 1 appears, with a
    broom, moving props around. Loud cheerful whistling. STAGEHAND 2
    appears, also with a broom.)

HERE SHE IS!

STAGEHAND 1. Hey Bert—wouldja get that crap from over there?
STAGEHAND 2. What crap, where?
STAGEHAND 1. The whadajacallit—
STAGEHAND 2. Flag?

(STAGEHAND 2 lifts the flag on its pedestal to carry backstage.)

STAGEHAND 2. What's this shit?

(He has found the MISS MICHIGN banner, a high-heeled shoe, and some false red-polished fingernails.)

STAGEHAND 2. *(Sliding the banner across his chest, fitting on a fingernail.)*Hey, look: woweee!

(In the meantime, STAGEHAND 1 has found MISS ALABAMA's glossy wig, which he fits crookedly on his head; and her padded bra, which he waves high.)

STAGEHAND 1. Woweee! Look at me! *(Wriggling hips,etc.)* "Miss America"!

(STAGEHAND 2 whistles, stamps feet. STAGEHAND return to work. Exit with props. A beat. Empty stage. BARBARA wanders in, still in her swim suit and high heels, MISS AMERICA banner across her breasts. She glances about in confusion and worry.)

BARBARA. Why am I...still here? *(A beat.)* This is a dream... isn't it? But I should be awake by now. It must be morning by now. *(Strikes heel against floor.)* But everything is so real. *(Discovers crown on head, banner across breasts.)* Oh, God! I'm staring to get frightened. *(Pause, pleading.)* Mom, if this is you, you can wake up now. Mom? Please?

(Lights slowly out.)

END OF PLAY

NEGATIVE

NEGATIVE was first performed at the Philadelphia Festival Theatre for New Plays, 1995.

CAST

MARY: *A young Caucasian woman*
VERONICA: *A young, black woman*

In this encounter, racial stereotypes are reversed, as in a photograph negative. The mood and pacing should suggest a comedy of which the participants are unaware

(LIGHTS UP. MARY has just entered the college dormitory room she will be sharing with another freshman woman. She is moderately attractive and modestly dressed; may wear glasses; wears a yellow freshman beanie and a shiny yellow identification button with HI! in black letters. The room is sparely furnished: two beds at opposite corners, two desks (one near a window), lamps, chairs, bureaus; two closets, doors shut. Clothes have been laid in neat piles across suitcases and cartons of books, shoes, etc. in the center of the room. VERONICA's possessions are considerably more lavish than MARY's; included is a hefty trunk.)

MARY. *(A naive childlike tone.)* So—this is it! At last! My freshman room! Oh God I'm so excited I can't stand it! The college of my choice—my dreams! And I'm here on a scholarship—they want me! *(Pause, hugs herself.)* For months I've been dreaming of this moment and now I'm here— alone. My roommate's been here—and gone out again—we haven't met—my folks are driving back to Davenport and I'm—here—alone. *(A touch of panic.)* For the first time in my life I will be—living away from home. A thousand miles away where no one knows me. Gosh, I'm scared. *(Thumb to mouth.)* Oh Mom!— Mommy! Daddy!—come back! *(Pause.)* No. I am not scared. I am MARY Strep, Class of 1998. Whooeee! *(Tiptoes over to examine her roommate's things.)* Oh, God!—my roommate must be rich. *(Holds a stylish leather miniskirt against herself; stares into a mirror on a wall.)* Wow. *(Holds up a dressier costume; sighs.)* Oh!—so pretty. *(She discovers a framed photograph of VERONICA and her family which she stares at appalled.)* Oh!—oh no. Oh no. The college has matched me with one of <u>them</u>.

(VERONICA strides into the room with a dazzling smile. Very attractive, self-assured. She too is wearing a freshman beanie but wears it with style; also a tight colorful college T-shirt, an eye-catching skirt. The HI! button is prominent on her breast. A beat as MARY and VERONICA stare at each other.)

VERONICA. *(Recovering first, exuding "personality".)* Well, hi! I'm Veronica Scott, your roommate!

NEGATIVE

MARY. Oh!—h-hi! *(She has almost dropped the photograph; stammers guiltily.)* I was j-just admiring your f-family—

VERONICA. *(Warmly extending her hand to shake MARY's.)* Please call me "Ronnie"—all my friends do.

MARY. *(Shyly and awkwardly shaking hands, as if it's a new things for her.)* "R-Ronnie"—

VERONICA. "Veronica" is a nice enough name but far too formal, don't you think? I believe in informality.

MARY. *(Nervous.)* Oh, yes—

VERONICA. I believe in egalitarianism.

MARY. "Egali—?" Oh, yes—

VERONICA. And what is your name?

MARY. My n-name?

VERONICA. Maybe it's on your name-tag?

MARY. *(Squinting down at the button.)* Oh yes—"Mary Strep."

VERONICA. "Mary Step."

MARY. "Strep."

VERONICA. "Step"?—that's what I said.

MARY. "Strep."

VERONICA. With your accent I'm having trouble hearing it. "Mary Strep"—?

MARY. Yes.

VERONICA. Hmmm!—"Mary Strep." I like it.

MARY. *(Faintly incredulous.)* You do?

VERONICA. Oh, yes! You don't hear many names like that. So—exotic. Musical. Is it a name with a legend?

MARY. I guess it's just a, a—name. Like in the telephone directory.

VERONICA. Oooooh no it isn't just a name, it's a—an aura. It has its own history, I bet.

MARY. My mother's name is "Mary" and so is my grandmother's—"Mary." Back through my father's family everybody is named "Strep."

VERONICA. *(Wide-eyed.)* Ooooh see what I mean!

MARY. *(A bit too eagerly.)* People call me "Mary"—for short.

VERONICA. Fascinating! And where are all these people?

MARY. Huh?

VERONICA. Sorry, I mean where are you from, Mary?

MARY. Davenport, Iowa.

VERONICA. Ooooh no! You aren't! *(Enunciates words sensuously.)* "Davenport, Iowa"!

MARY. What's wrong?

NEGATIVE

VERONIVA. Nothing's wrong, it's just you're the first person from Davenport, Iowa I've ever met.

MARY. Gosh, I'm sorry...

VERONICA. oh, no—it's fabulous. "Davenport, Iowa." Such a wholesome cereal-sounding kind of place! *(Pause, sighs.)* I'm from Greenwich, Connecticut: quintessence of American Suburbia.

MARY. "Greenwich, Connecticut"—I've heard of it, I think. It sounds beautiful. So—green?

VERONICA. And where did you go to high school. Mary?

MARY. *(Surprised.)* In Davenport, Iowa.

VERONICA. Oh—there's a school there?

MARY. *(Puzzled.)*Sure. Davenport High School.

VERONICA. *(Catching on.)*Oh, I see!—public school. You went to public school—of course.

MARY. Where—did you go?

VERONICA. *(Airily.)*Oh, Exeter. Eight members of our graduating class are here as freshmen; must be twenty-five Exeter grads on campus. Can't escape us!

MARY. Exeter must be— an exclusive school?

VERONICA. Oooooh no! Not really. We had lots of scholarship students. Exeter is racially mixed, and balanced; two of my closest friends—and a roommate, junior year—were white girls. Really.

MARY. That's...nice.

VERONICA. *(Proudly.)* The president of our senior class was a white boy.

MARY. Oh that's...nice.

VERONICA. And he was gay; and he had psoriasis. We all loved him.

MARY. ...nice...

VERONICA. At least, he's not here. *(Pause; rubbing hands together briskly.)* Well! Which corner of the room would you prefer, Mary? I was here earlier but I deliberately didn't choose, I thought I'd leave the choice to you.

MARY. To me?

VERONICA. Why, yes!—to you. That corner has the window, and that corner has the, um, corner.

MARY. *(Shyly.)* Gosh, I—just don't know.

VERONICA: A view of the bell tower and the historic green where a climactic battle of the Revolutionary War was fought— or a view of the, um, corner?

MARY. *(Very hesitantly pointing toward the window.)* Well— maybe— if you don't m-mind—

NEGATIVE

VERONICA: My, thanks! *(As if MARY has pointed in the reverse direction, VERONICA takes the bed near the window; she speaks sincerely.)* Now you're sure, Mary? You don't mind not having the view, or any natural light?

MARY. *(Swallowing.)* I guess not...Veronica.

VERONICA. *(Shaking forefinger, big smile.)* Now, now—"Ronnie"!

MARY. "R-Ronnie."

VERONICA. I'll call you "Mary,"—I adore that name!—if you'll call me "Ronnie." *(Places a quilted spread on her bed as if to claim it.)* Now: the closets. Which is your preference, Mary?

MARY. *(Squinting and groping about.)* It's sort of...dark... over here. I don't see a closet.

VERONICA. The big, spacious one is back beyond your desk; the absurdly cramped one is over here by mine. But please feel free to choose whichever you wish.

MARY. Oh, now I see it! *(Opens closet door.)* Gee, it is spacious.

VERONICA. Obviously, I have many more clothes and suit cases than you do, Mary, but—it's your choice.

MARY. *(Apologetically.)* It probably makes sense for me to take this one, Ronnie, doesn't it?—since it's—

VERONICA. *(Sharply.)* What'd you call me, girl?

MARY. "R-Ronnie"—

VERONICA. Oh, right—I guess I told you to call me "Ronnie." *(Slightly forced smile.)* If we're going to be roommates I suppose it's best to be—informal. *(Tapping foot impatiently.)* Take your time choosing, Mary. We've got all afternoon.

MARY. *(Shyly.)* Well, like I said it probably makes sense for me to take this closet, since it's right beside my—

VERONICA. *(Now a sincere dazzling smile.)* Oh, that's sweet of you, Mary!—thanks.

(Again VERONICA behaves as if MARY has said exactly the reverse of what she has said. VERONICA begins to hang up her clothes in the larger closet; MARY has no choice but to hang up her clothes in the other closet.)

VERONICA. We'll have dinner together, Mary, O.K.? You can join me and my friends from Exeter—and these really cool guys I just met. Unless you have other plans?

MARY. *(Quickly.)* Oh no, no—I don't know anyone here. It's such a big place and I—I don't know anyone here.

NEGATIVE

VERONICA. *(Squeezing MARY's hand.)* Well, you know me.

(As MARY goes to hang up a dress, VERONICA pauses to admire it effusively. It is a quite ordinary plaid wool dress with a white bow, white cuffs.)

VERONICA. Ooooh! What is this?

MARY. *(Shyly.)* My good wool dress...

VERONICA. Good Will dress?

MARY. Good wool dress.

VERONICA. Where'd you find such a—style?

MARY. My grandma sewed it for me. For my eighteenth birthday just two weeks ago.

VERONICA. No! Your grandmother sewed this?— *(Making a sewing gesture as if plying a needle.)* —by hand?

MARY. Oh, no, Grandma uses a sewing machine—a Singer. She's had the same identical machine since 1938.

VERONICA. No! You don't say!

MARY. Grandma sewed my senior prom gown, too—sixty yards of pink taffeta and chiffon; and strapless! *(A bit daringly.)*

VERONICA. My grandmothers, they insist we grandchildren call them "Meredith" and "Tracey"—their first names. They look young as my mother. *(Laughs.)* They'd as soon run a sewing machine as a—butter churn. I'm envious! *(Holding MARY's dress against herself, admiring.)*

MARY. *(Proudly.)* Actually, Grandma sews all my clothes. She sewed these. *(Indicating the nondescript outfit she is wearing.)*

VERONICA. Isn't that sweet! Soooo caring: Must be a folkway, or something? In Indiana?

MARY. *(Shyly.)* What's a—folkway?

VERONICA. *(Airily intellectual.)* Oh, just some species of unexamined ethnic, religious, or regional custom aborigines persist in practicing over the centuries without a clue as to why. Claude Levi-Strauss is still the most insightful analyst of the phenomenon. *(Preening before mirror.)* You see, Mary, when you wear this um, most original dress your grandmother sewed for you, you feel happy because you feel loved. That's a folkway.

MARY. Oh. *(Wipes at eyes.)* Gosh, I'm going to m-miss Grandma—so far away!

VERONICA. You see?—emotion of a primitive, visceral, binding nature is generated out of, um, not much. *(Examining dress, turns a sleeve roughly inside out.)* How's this sewed together?—oh! *(She has ripped a seam.)*

MARY. *(Recoiling as if feeling pain.)* Oh!

NEGATIVE

VERONICA. *(Sincerely.)* Gee, I'm sorry, Mary.

(MARY tries to take the dress from VERONICA, but VERONICA retains it.)

MARY. *(Childlike, accusing.)* You ripped the seam, Veronica...
VERONICA. It was an accident, Mary. I said I was sorry.
MARY. You tugged at it, I saw you.
VERONICA. I did not tug, I possibly pulled. The thread is rotted—see? *(Tugs slightly, and another seam rips.)* Sub-standard.
MARY. *(Pain.)* Oh! Grandma!—

(MARY takes the dress from VERONICA, staggering to her side of the room;
contemplates the dress; hangs it in the closet. VERONICA has located a
camera amid her possessions, and approaches MARY.)

VERONICA. Mary?—turn here!

(MARY turns, and VERONICA takes a quick flash photo.)

VERONICA. Thanks, Mary! That's cool.
MARY. *(A bit blinded.)* W-What did you do that for?
VERONICA. *(A bit evasively.)* Um—just wanted to. I'm sentimental. This being our first day together, and all. *(Pause, warmly.)* Mary, I know! I'll have your dress mended by this wonderful French seamstress who sews my Momma's clothes. She can replace all that rotted old thread with new. And, um, maybe straighten the hemline...
MARY. *(Quickly.)* No, thanks—I'll take the dress home at Thanksgiving, and Grandma can mend it herself. She'd want to.
VERONICA. I just hope these quaint old Midwestern folkways don't die out before Thanksgiving!
MARY. *(Coolly.)* If you mean my Grandma Crockett, she's only eighty-three years old. Her mother is still alive and going strong with her Singer Sewing machine— *(Proudly.)* —at the age of one hundred and one.
VERONICA. *(Genuinely amazed.)* No! You actually have a great-grandmother, Mary?—one hundred one years old?
MARY. Great-grandma Quantril is my younger great-grandmother, in fact.
VERONICA. Ooooh! I just have to record this! *(She has located a tape recorder amid her possessions; slips in a cassette, sets the machine going.)* You say, Mary, you have two great-grandmothers?—and how many grandmothers?

NEGATIVE

MARY. *(Staring at recorder.)* W-What is that?

VERONICA. Oh, probably you don't have these in Indiana—don't pay the slightest heed.

MARY. You're—recording what I say? R-right now?

VERONICA. No, no it's nothing! Don't mind me.

MARY. But—

VERONICA. Just a little hobby of mine. Like say a guy calls me, I have the recorder hooked up to the phone, I set it going—for fun.

MARY. But makes me n-nervous, Veronica. I wish you'd turn it off.

VERONICA. I said—never mind me, you're the fascinating one of the two of us, Mary. Rich archival lore! *(Mysteriously.)* I see I have much, much to learn this freshman year, Now, about the grandmothers—

MARY. *(A bit stiffly.)* I'd rather not discuss my grandmothers any more right now, thanks. "Ronnie."

VERONICA. Oh, but think of those old pioneer women out there on the great cereal plains of America—sewing away. Gives me the shivers!

MARY. Actually...Davenport is a city.

VERONICA. "Davenport"—what's that?

MARY. Where I'm from—Davenport, Ohio. I mean—Iowa. It's city, not a cereal field. *(A bit boastful.)* We have a population of over 100,000.

VERONICA. *(Skeptical.)* People?

MARY. Yes...

VERONICA. *(Catching on.)* Oh, you mean white people.

MARY. *(Noticing tape recorder.)* Gosh, is that thing still on?

VERONICA. No! *(Pretends to be switching the recorder off.)* There we are: off. *(Teasing.)* My, we're a little thin-skinned, Mary, aren't we? That's how Davenportians are?

MARY. I'm s-sorry, it just makes me nervous—

VERONICA. You know, Mary, your accent is so interesting. I've never heard one quite like it before.

MARY. My accent?

VERONICA. *(Laughs.)* Hear? The way you say "accent"...

MARY. How is it supposed to sound?

VERONICA. *(An English intonation.)* "Ac-cent."

MARY. *(Nasal.)* "Ac-cent." "Ac-cent."

(VERONICA tries to hide her laughter.)

MARY. *(Hurt.)* What's so f-funny?

VERONICA. Not a thing. I adore the way you talk, Mary!

NEGATIVE

MARY. *(Perplexed.)* Up until a few days ago, when we left home to drive East, I never had the slightest accent. Nobody did! I don't know how on earth I got one here.

VERONICA. *(Hands to mouth but snorting with laughter.)* Oh! there you go again!

MARY. What? What?

(VERONICA squeals with laughter as if she's being tickled; then forces herself to become sober.)

VERONICA. Mary, look: America is a mosaic of many, many different ways of speech—local customs—"ac-cents"— *(She cruelly imitates MARY's "accent".)*—it's a democracy and we're all equal.

MARY. We are?

(VERONICA stifles laughter again.)

MARY. *(Miserably.)* Everybody's going to laugh at me here— I know it. My professors, my classmates, my r-roomate— In my dreams, all summer, I'd hear strangers laughing at me— but I didn't know why.

VERONICA. *(Practicably.)* Well, now you know. That's a gain.

MARY. Maybe you could h-help me, Ronnie? I could learn to talk like you?

VERONICA. *(Graciously.)* I have no objections if you try to model yourself after me, certainly. My little, um, white girl roommate at Exeter tried that, too. It was such fun.

MARY. What happened?

VERONICA. Oh, I don't know. We were just roommates a few weeks before she, um, dropped out of school. Vanished without a trace.

MARY. *(Upset.)* Is that recorder-thing still on?

VERONICA. It is not. I told you I turned it off, didn't I?

MARY. Why is this little wheel still going round?

VERONICA. It's unwinding. Relax. Mary.

(MARY would turn back to continue unpacking, but VERONICA detains her. An initial shyness, or a pretense of shyness, on VERONICA's part.)

VERONICA. Oh, er...Mary? Now we've, um, gotten to know each other so well...can I ask you something personal?

MARY. *(Guardedly.)* What?

NEGATIVE

VERONICA. Your hair.

MARY. *(Touching hair, alarmed.)* My hair? That's a question?

VERONICA. Promise, now, you won't be miffed?—you're kind of thin-skinned, I've discovered.

MARY. I won't...be miffed.

VERONICA. Promise!

MARY. *(With dread.)* I promise.

VERONICA. I've always wanted to ask one of you: is your hair naturally that way?

MARY. What way?

VERONICA. Or do you do something to it?

MARY. How—is it?

(VERONICA touches MARY's hair with cautious fingers; her expression is one of someone touching an insect.)

VERONICA. So sort of—fine. Dry. Ooooh!—sort of shivery.

MARY. *(Backing off.)* I d-don't do anything to my hair except shampoo it.

VERONICA. Don't you brush it? comb it?

MARY. *(Hotly.)* Of course I brush and comb it! I just don't think about it.

VERONICA. *(Faint protest.)* But your hair is—lovely, Mary. It suits you perfectly.

MARY. I—I 'd better finish packing, I mean unpacking... *(Fumblingly returns to her things.)*

VERONICA. *(Cheerfully.)* I'd better finish unpacking. We have a date for dinner, remember?—a big table of us. You'll love my friends, Mary. And I know they'll be crazy about you. *(Pause.)*

(MARY is so rattled she drops something; VERONICA doesn't notice.)

VERONICA. And these two guys I just met—are they cool.

(MARY and VERONICA are busily hanging up clothes, unpacking suitcases and boxes. etc.)

MARY. *(Worried.)* These guys, um—are they?—

VERONICA. Seniors. Real hunks!

MARY. Are they, er—?

VERONICA. Good-looking? You bet!

NEGATIVE

MARY. I mean, um—

VERONICA. Tall? For sure. I don't go out with dwarfs!

MARY. *(Miserably nervous.)* I, er, was wondering what— r-r-race—

VERONICA. *(Surprised.)* "Race"—?

MARY. I mean, you know—what c-c-color—their skin—

VERONICA. "Color"?—skin"? *(A beat.)* I didn't notice.

MARY. Oh.

VERONICA. I never notice such superfluities. Race-skin— color: America is a mosaic, we're all absolutely equal, we're beyond primitive divisions of us and them.

MARY. Yes, but I—I get n-nervous, if— I mean, I don't feel comfortable if— I had this feeling, when my folks and I crossed the quad, and came into the dorm here—p-people were watching us.

VERONICA. What kind of people?

MARY. The, uh—majority people. Your people.

VERONICA. Mary, that isn't so! Why'd anybody look at you? *(Pause, embarrassed.)* Oh, um—I didn't mean that the way it sounded. I just meant— people like you are 100% welcome here—this college has been integrated since 1978! Wasn't that a rousing speech the Chancellor gave this morning?— "Giving a Boost to The Needy." And you "Deficiency Scholars" aren't tagged in any obvious way; it's almost as if you scored high SATs and your folks can pay full tuition like the rest of us. Really.

MARY. *(Thumb to mouth.)* R-Really?

VERONICA. Roommates are warned—I mean, notified—but only so we can help tutor you, if necessary. I volunteered to room with one of you, for that purpose.

MARY. Gee, you did?

VERONICA. Well, it fits in with my Freshman Honors Seminar thesis.

MARY. *(Stunned.)* You've chosen your topic already? What is it?

VERONICA. Um...a photo-journal account. Kind of a personal diary, With anthropological and psychological dimensions, of course.

MARY. You're going to write about...me?

VERONICA. Oh no, oh no!—don't be silly, Mary. Not you. Not you personally.

MARY. Now I feel kind of...funny.

VERONICA. Well, you wouldn't, if you didn't take everything so personally! *(Pause.)* Just be yourself. Be your natural self. That's my philosophy of life.

MARY. *(Swallowing hard.)* "Just be yourself." I'll try, Ver-, "Ronnie." Can I model myself after you?

NEGATIVE

VERONICA. Oooooh is that sweet! *(Gives MARY a quick kiss on the cheek, which quite dazes MARY.)* But you should just be you, if you know who that is. That's what growing up in America in these enlightened times is all about.

(MARY and VERONICA continue unpacking, etc. VERONICA removes her beanie and tosses it onto her bed; MARY, watching her imitates her— but MARY's beanie misses her bed. VERONICA whistles and moves to suggestive dance music; MARY imitates her, unable to do more than hiss, and moving about most clumsily.)

VERONICA. Um—Mary?
MARY. *(Eager, yet in dread.)* Y-Yes, "Ronnie"?
VERONICA. Could you do me a favor and carry this trunk downstairs to the storage room?

(A beat.)

VERONICA. *(Radiant smile.)* I'll be happy to pay you, of course!
MARY. *(Stunned.)* N-Now?
VERONICA. Well, before dinner. Is $5 enough?
MARY. I...
VERONICA. $10?
MARY. But I...

(VERONICA locates her wallet, takes out a $10 bill, lays it on MARY's desk with a flourish.)

VERONICA. Thanks so much, Mary. I appreciate it. *(Pause.)* These suitcases, now—hmmm!—maybe they can fit into your closet?
MARY. S-Suitcases? Gosh, I don't think so—
VERONICA. *(Peering into MARY's closet, shoving clothes on hangers roughly aside.)* Well, we can try. C'mon, help me. *(VERONICA and MARY push several of VERONICA's suit cases into the closet.)* Tight fit, but it's O.K. Thanks!

(Some of MARY's shoes have been forced out of the closet; MARY, not know ing what to do with them, puts them beneath her bed. VERONICA is unnoticing.)

NEGATIVE

MARY. *(Plaintively.)* But, Veronica, here are my own s-suitcases—

VERONICA. You can take them down to the storage with you, along with my trunk. They're made of cardbook, not leather— they won't scratch. What's the problem? *(Genuinely puzzled.)*

(MARY stands stunned for a beat or two; then begins feebly complying with VERONICA's order, carrying/dragging the suitcases and the trunk to the door. During this speech of VERONICA 's she moves like an automaton, more and more slowly.)

VERONICA. *(Shyly boastful.)*I didn't want to, um, overwhelm you right off, Mary, but...my father is Byron T. Scott. *(No response from MARY.)* Yes, that's right!—I'm the daughter of Byron T. Scott himself. *(Pause.)* Daddy is in private practice in Manhattan now, but, in the Sixties, I guess you know, he was a renowned civil rights attorney, A personal friend of John F. Kennedy— and Jackie; and, now, Bill and Hilary. *(Pause; no response from MARY, but VERONICA behaves as if there is.)* Yes, I sure am lucky, Mary! And I know it. Daddy was a champion of integration from the first. In his law firm he always hires whites—not by quota, either. And the handicapped. *(Pause.)* Physically and mentally challenged—Daddy doesn't discriminate, nor does he allow others to do so. Ooooh no! That's how we were brought up.

(MARY continues to move more and more slowly.)

VERONICA. *(Lyric, sentimental.)*Mary, I want to share this with you. One of my earliest memories is of my nanny... who was white. *(Pause.)* Nellie Fay Cotton, the kindly, obese, diabetic Ozark woman my parents hired at the minimum wage to care for me when I was just a baby. Ooooh did I love Nellie Fay! She was ugly as sin, and, ugh, the ugliest hair but her soul was beautiful inside. *(Pause.)* Nellie was of welfare stock—had fifteen children by the age of thirty-five— her husband was an unemployed miner with black lung who had nothing to do all day but drink and beat up on her till she finally escaped with her children and fled North—but Nellie never lost her faith in God— never! "The Lord sees into our hearts, He loves us each and every one"— Nelle used to tell me, when I was still in my crib. *(Wiping at eyes, maudlin.)* Then, one summer when I was five or six, these sort of snooty relatives of Momma's were visiting, from Boston, and my aunt's sapphire choker was missing from her room, and Nellie Fay was the suspect of course, and oh! it was so sad!—Nellie Fay was scared and nervous and acted guilty—poor thing! The Green- wich police were called—interrogated Nellie down at the

NEGATIVE

station—did a body check, I guess—didn't find the missing jewelry—but Nellie Fay was dismissed from our household, and went away, and a few days later guess what?—

(VERONICA turns dramatically to MARY, who has come to a full halt, glassy-eyed and staring.)

VERONICA. You guessed it, Mary!—the damn old choker was found in the deep end of our swimming pool, when the maintenance men came to clean it. Oh, were Momma and Daddy apologetic! oh, were they chagrined! Right away they sent for Nellie Fay, but it was too late. Poor dear Nellie had killed herself—in shame—swallowed a can of Drano she'd taken out of our kitchen. Oh! the sorrow in our household! the regret! It took Momma weeks and weeks to find an adequate replacement!

(MARY rouses herself, goes to the dress VERONICA has torn, and begins mending it; again, like an automaton. She no longer seems conscious of VERONICA. Telephone rings. VERONICA answers it excitedly.)

VERONICA. *(Exuding "personality".)* Hi! Yeah! *(Listens.)* What?—oh, wow! Cool! Tonight? Dewitt, Evander, Jacey?— and Buchanan? Down from New Haven? Hmmmm! How many cars? To Manhattan? *(As if indecisive.)* When? *(Pause.)* Buchanan's got his Jag? Oooh, count me in. *(Listens.)* No, no—what other plans would I have for tonight? This place is Dullsville. Bye! *(Hangs up.)*

MARY sits on her bed, mending her dress as before.

VERONICA. *(Now noticing.)* Ohhhh! An extant aboriginal folkway—in my room. *(Hurries to adjust camera)* Mary, don't pay the slightest attention to me, hmmm? Just keep right on! This will be an intimate shot of both of us—to commemorate our first day together. The frontispiece of my photo-journal... Now, I set this mechanism here—O.K.! *(Hurries to get into the picture, squeezing in beside MARY on the bed; her arm around MARY's shoulders and her head close beside MARY's.)* Oh are we going to have a terrific freshman year! One-two- three SMILE!

(VERONICA smiles her dazzling smile; MARY is now catatonic again though managing to smile a slow, ghastly, blank smile for the camera. Camera flashes.)

NEGATIVE

(Lights out.)

END OF PLAY

THE ADOPTION

THE ADOPTION was first performed at Ensemble Studio Theatre, New York City, 1996.

CAST

MR.: *A Caucasian man in his late 30's or early 40's*
MRS.: *A Caucasian woman of about the same age*
X: *Male or female, of any mature age*
NABBO: *A child*
NADBO: *A "twin" of NABBO*

SETTING

An adoption agency office. Sterile surroundings, merely functional furnishings. Prominent on the wall facing the audience is a large clock with a minute hand of the kind that visibly "jumps" from minute to minute. At the start, the clock measures real time by subtle degrees, it begins to accelerate.

TIME

The Present

(LIGHTS UP. We have been hearing bright, cheery music ("It's a Lovely Day Today") which now subsides. MR. and MRS. are seated side by side, gripping hands; they appear excited and apprehensive. They are conventionally well-dressed, as if for church, and do indeed exude a churchy aura. MR. has brought a briefcase, MRS. a "good" purse. A large bag (containing children's toys) close by. To the left of MR. and MRS. is a door in the wall; to the right, behind them, is the clock. With LIGHTS UP the clock begins its ticking, the time at 11:00..)

MRS. I'm so excited—frightened!

MR. It's the day we've been waiting for—I'm sure.

MRS. Oh, do you think—? I don't dare to hope.

MR. They were encouraging, last time—

MRS. Yes, they were!

MR. They wouldn't send us away empty-handed again—would they?

MRS. Well, they did last time, and the time before last—

MR. But this is going to be different, I'm sure. They hinted—

MRS. No, they all but said—promised—

MR. —um, not a promise exactly, but—

MRS. It was, it was a promise!—almost. In all but words.

MR. Yes. They hinted—today is the day.

MRS. *(On her feet, too excited to remain seated.)* The day we've been awaiting—for so long!

MR. *(On his feet)* So long!

MRS. I feel like a, a bride again! A—virgin! *(Giggles.)*

MR. (Touching or embracing her.) You look like a madonna.

MRS. It's a, a—delivery—

MR. *(Subtle correction.)* A deliverance.

MRS. *(Euphoric, intense.)* We can't just live for ourselves alone. A woman, a man—

MR. *(Emphatically.)* That's selfish.

MRS. That's—unnatural.

MR. Lonely.

MRS. *(Wistfully.)* So lonely.

MR. A home without—

75

THE ADOPTION

MRS. —children—

MR. —is empty.

MRS. Not what you'd call a "home"—

MR. But we have means, we can afford to "extend our boundaries."

MRS. Thank God! *(Eyes uplifted, sincerely.)*

MR. *(Glance upward.)* Yes, indeed—thank You, God. *(Pause.)* Of course, um—we're not millionaires. Just, um—"comfortable."

MRS. —"comfortable Americans"—

MR. —of the "educated" class—"middle class"—

MRS. Oh, dear—aren't we "upper-middle"? Your salary—

MR. *(Finger to lips, stern.)* We are not millionaires.

MRS. Well-we've "paid off our mortgage," we have a "tidy little nest egg", we've made "sensible, long-term investments"—

MR. *(Cautioning.)* We are what you'd call medium comfortable. We can afford to extend our boundaries, and begin a—family.

MRS. *(Almost tearful.)* A family! After twelve years of waiting!

MR. *(Counting rapidly on fingers.)* Um—thirteen, darling.

MRS. *(Belatedly realizing what she has said.)* I mean—twelve years of marriage. Not just waiting. *(Glances at MR..)* Oh—thirteen?

MR. *(Defensive.)* We've been happy, of course. Our marriage hasn't been merely waiting—

MRS. —for a, a baby—

MR. —a family—

MRS. *(Cradling gesture with her arms.)*—a darling little baby—

MR. —strapping young son—

MRS. *(Emphatically.)* We've done plenty of other things!

MR. Certainly have! Hobbies, travel— *(A bit blank.)* —paying off our mortgage—

MRS. *(Grimly.)* We've been happy. We love each other, after all.

MR. Sure do! Sweetest gal in the world! *(Kisses MRS.'s cheek.)*

MRS. *(Repeating in same tone.)* We've been happy.

MR. Damned happy.

MRS. We have snapshots to prove it—

MR. Albums of snapshots to prove it!

(A pause. MR. and MRS. glance nervously at the clock.)

MRS. *(A soft voice.)* Of course, every now and then—

MR. —in the interstices of happiness—

MRS. —between one heartbeat and the next—

THE ADOPTION

MR. —in the early, insomniac hours of the morning, maybe—
MRS. —in the bright-lit maze of the food store—
MR.—like fissures of deep, sharp shadow at noon—
MRS. we have sometimes, for maybe just a—
MR. —fleeting second—
MRS. —teensy-weensy fleeting second—
MR. —been a bit lonely.

(Pause.)

MRS. *(Sad, clear voice.)* So lonely.

(Pause.)

(The door opens, and X appears. X is a bureaucrat, in conventional office attire; may wear rimless glasses; carries a clipboard containing numerous documents. He/She is impersonally "friendly.")

X. *(Bright smile, loud voice.)* Goooood morning!*(Consults clip board.)* You are—Mr. and Mrs.—?
MR., MRS. *(Excited, hopeful.)* That's right! *(MRS. quickly straightens MR.'s necktie, which has become crooked.)*
X. *(Making a production of shaking hands.)* Mr.—! Mrs.—! Soooo glad to meet you.
MRS. *(Flushed, hand to bosom.)* So g-glad to meet you.
MR. Is this the— *(Fearful of asking "is this the day".)* —the right time?
X. No time like the present! That's agency policy.
MRS. An—excellent policy.
MR. *(Nodding.)* Very excellent.
X. And you're punctual, Mr. and Mrs.—, I see. A good sign.
MR.. Oh, we're very punctual.
MRS. *(Breathless.)* Always have been!
MR. We've been here since 7:45 A.M., actually. When the custodial staff unlocked the building.
MRS. We came to the c-city last night. We're staying in a hotel.
MR. —a medium-priced hotel!—
MRS. We were terrified of missing our appointment—
MR. *(Chiding MRS.)* We were not terrified, we were—vigilant.
MRS. Yes, vigilant—
X. It is wise to be punctual. Such details in perspective parents are

THE ADOPTION

meticulously noted. *(Mysteriously taps documents.)*

MR. *(A deep breath.)* And is today the d-day?

MRS. *(A hand on MR.'s arm, faintly echoing.)*—the d-day?

X. *(Beaming.)* Yes. Today is your day, Mr. and Mrs.—. Your application to adopt one of our orphans has been fully processed by our board of directors, and approved. Congratulations!

MRS. Oh—! Oh!

MR.. Oh my God!

(MR. and MRS. clasp hands, thrilled. X strides to the door, opens it with a flourish, and leads in NABBO.)

X. Here he is, Mr. and Mrs.—your baby.

MR., MRS.. *(Faintly.)* "Our baby!"

(NABBO is perhaps eight years old. He wears a mask to suggest deformity or disfigurement, but the mask should be extremely lifelike and not exaggerated. His skin is an ambiguous tone— dusky or mottled, not "black." He may be partly bald as well, as if his scalp has been burnt. He has a mild twitch or tremor. MR. and MRS. stare at NABBO, who stares impassively at them.)

X. *(Rubbing hands together.)* So! Here we are! Here we have "Nabbo." *(Nudging him.)* Say hello to your new mother and father, Nabbo.

(NABBO is silent.)

MR., MRS. H-Hello!

X. *(A bit coercive.)* Say "Hello: to your new mother and father, Nabbo. "Hel-lo."

(NABBO is silent.)

MR. *(Hesitantly.)* He isn't a, an actual—baby—is he?

X. *(Consulting document.)* Nabbo is eight months old. To the day.

MR. Eight months—?

MRS. Oh but he's—so sweet. So—

X. Our records are impeccable.

MRS. —childlike, So—

MR.. *(A bit doubtful, to X.)* What did you say his name is?

THE ADOPTION

MRS. —trusting. So—
X. "Nabbo." "NAB-BO." (Equal stress on both syllables)
MRS. —needful of our love!

(X pushes NABBO toward MR. nd MRS. He is weakly resistant.)

MR., MRS. "Nab-bo"—?
X. *(Brightly urging NABBO.)* 'Hel-lo!"

(NABBO remains silent. Visible tremor.)

MR. Maybe he doesn't know—English?
MRS. Of course he doesn't, that's the problem. *(Speaking loudly, brightly.)* Hel-lo, Nab-bo! You've come a long distance to us, haven't you? Don't be frightened. We are your new Mommy and your Daddy— *(Points to herself and to MR..)* We'll teach you everything you need to know.
MR.: We sure will!

(MR. has taken a camera out of his briefcase and takes pictures of MRS. posing with NABBO. NABBO is rigid with terror of the flash.)

MR.. Beau-ti-ful! The first minute of our new life. *(Takes another picture.)*
MRS.. This is a holy time. I feel God's presence here.
MR. *(To X, hesitantly.)* Excuse me, but is Nabbo a, um—little boy, or a little girl?
MRS. *(Gently poking MR..)* Dear, don't be crude!
MR.. I'm only curious.
X. *(Checking document, frowning.)* You didn't specify, did you? You checked "either sex."
MRS. *(Eagerly.)* Oh yes, oh yes! "Either."
MR. *(Protesting.)* Hey, I was just curious. I'm Daddy, after all.
MRS.. *(Fussing over NABBO, squatting beside him.)* He's "Daddy," dear; and I'm "Mommy." We've waited so long for you! Only for you, dear. Can you say "Daddy"—"Mommy"?

(NABBO remains silent, twitching slightly.)

MR. *(As if NABBO is deaf.)* "DAD-DY"—"MOM-MY"—
MRS. *(Her ear to NABBO's mouth, but hears nothing.)* Of course, you're shy; you've come such a long distance.

THE ADOPTION

MR. *(Solemnly.)* From the "dark side of the Earth."

MRS. *(To MR., chiding.)*Don't be so—grim, dear. That isn't the right tone. *(To NABBO; singing.)* "Little Baby Bunting! Daddy's gone a-hunting! Gone to get a new fur skin! To wrap the Baby Bunting in!"

MR.. *(Joining in.)* "—wrap the Baby Bunting in!" *(Laughs, rubs hands happily together)* I can't believe this is real.

MRS. . *(To NABBO.)* Now, Naddo—

MR. "Nab-bo"—

MRS. That's what I said: "Nad-do."

MR. Dear, it's "Nab-bo."

MRS: "Nab-bo"? That's what I said. My goodness! *(She turns to the bag, removing a large doll from it.)* Look, Nabbo darling—just for you. Isn't she lovely? *(Urging NABBO to take the doll, but NABBO is motionless, not lifting his/her arms.)*

MR. *(Taking a shiny toy firetruck out of the bag; in a hearty "masculine" voice.)* Nabbo, look what Daddy has for you. Cool, eh? *(Running the truck vigorously along the floor, making "engine" noises deep in his throat.)* RRRRRRRMMMMMMMM! Cool, Nabbo, eh?

X. *(Holding out the clipboard and a pen.)* Excuse me, "Mommy" and"Daddy": please sign on the dotted line, and Nabbo is yours forever.

MRS. Oh, yes!

MR. Of course!

(As MR. takes the pen to sign, however, X suddenly draws back. As if he/she has just remembered.)

X. Um—one further detail.

MR., MRS. Yes? What?

X. It appears that-Nabbo has a twin.

MR., MRS.. *(Blankly.)* A—twin?

X. From whom Nabbo is said to be inseparable.

MR., MRS. "Inseparable"—?

X. They must be adopted together, you see.

MR., MRS. *(Trying to comprehend.)* Twin—?

(The minute hand of the clock continues to accelerate.)

X. Yes. An identical twin.

MR.. Identical? Like our c-child?

X. Frequently, our adoptees are from large lit- *(About to say "litter",*

THE ADOPTION

changes his/her mind.) —families. *(Pause.)* The term "twin" is merely generic.

MRS. I don't understand. Isn't our Nabbo one of a kind?

MR.. But—what does that mean?

MRS. "Inseparable—"?

(Pause. MR., MRS. stare at each other.)

MR. *(Suddenly, extravagant.)* Hell, I'm game! *(Throws arms wide.)*

MRS. *(Squeals with excitement, kneeling before NABBO.)* You have a twin, Nabbo? Another just like you?

MR. *(Recklessly.)* Two for the price of one, eh?

MRS. *(Faint, laughing, peering up at MR..)* Oh, but—"Daddy"—are we prepared? We've never had one, and now—two?

MR. Isn't that the way twins always come—in twos? Surprising Mommy and Daddy? *(Laughs.)*

MRS. *(Dazed euphoric.)* Oh yes oh yes oh yes! *(Pause, voice drops.)* I'm afraid.

(Pause.)

MR. I'm afraid. Gosh.

X. I regret to say, Mr. and Mrs.—, that our agency requires, in such a situation, that adoptive parents take in both siblings. For, given the fact of "identical twins," there can be no justification in adopting one instead of the other.

MRS.. That's...so.

MR. *(Wiping face with handkerchief.)* You got us there...yes!

(X takes NABBO's arm as if to lead him back through the door.)

X. *(Somber voice.)* There are so many deserving applicants registered with our agency, you see. Our waiting list is years long.

MRS. *(Desperate.)* Oh—oh, wait—

MR.. Hey, wait—

MRS. *(Hugging NABBO.)* We want them both—of course.

MR. *(Wide, dazed grin.)* I'm game! —Did I say that?

X. *(Severely.)* You're certain, Mr. and Mrs.—?

MR., MRS.. Yes! Yes!

(X goes to the door, opens it and leads in NABBO, with some ceremony.)

THE ADOPTION

This, Mr. and Mrs—, is "Nabd-bo."

    MR., MRS. *(A bit numbed.)* "NAD-BOO."

    X. "NAD-BO."

    MR., MRS.. "NAD-BO."

(NABBO and NADBO, twins, stand side by side. They exhibit identical twitches and tremors, cowering together.)

    MRS.. *(Voice airy, strange.)* What a long long distance you have come to us—Nab-bo, Nad-bo! Yet we were fated.

    MR. From "the dark side of the Earth"—from "the beginning of time."

(MR., MRS. behave like doting parents, fussing over the twins.)

    MRS.. We'll teach you the English language—

    MR.. American English language—greatest language on Earth!

    MRS.. We'll bring you to our home—

    MR.. Your home, now—

    MRS. We'll love love love you so you forget whatever it is— *(Pause, a look of distaste.)* —you've escaped.

    MR.. That's for sure! No looking back.

    MRS.. No looking back, you'll be American children. No past!

    MR.. We're your new Mommy and Daddy—know what that means?

    MRS. *(Pointing.)* He's"Daddy"—I'm "Mommy"—

    MR. *(Overlapping, hearty.)* I'm "Mommy"—he's "Daddy"—

    MRS. *(Lightly chiding.)* I'm "Mommy."

    MR. *(Quickly.)* I mean—I', "Daddy." Of course!

    MRS.. *(Taking out of the bag a cap with bells.)* I knitted this myself, for you! *(Pause.)* Oh dear—there's only one. *(MRS. fits the cap awkwardly on NABBO's head; takes out a sweater.)* Thank goodness, I knitted this, too—

(NADBO takes the sweater from her, puts it over his head.)

    MR.. You'll have to knit matching sets, dear. From now on everything must be in duplicate.

    X. *(Smiling, but with authority.)* Hmmm! I do need your signatures, Mr. and Mrs.—, before the adoption procedure can continue.

(MR. wheels in a tricyle. Both children snatch at it, push at each other. The child who gets it, however, has no idea what it is, and struggles with it,

THE ADOPTION

knocking it over, attacking the wheels. MR. pulls in a wagon. Similar action.)

MRS. Oh!—I nearly forgot. You must be starving—having come so far! *(Takes fudge out of bag.)* I made this chocolate-walnut fudge just yesterday!

(NABBO, NADBO take pieces of proffered fudge; taste it hesitantly; begin to eat, ravenously; spit mouthfuls out.)

MRS.. Oh, dear! *(With a handkerchief, dabbing at their faces.)* You mustn't be greedy, you know. There's plenty to eat here.

(NABBO, NADBO snatch at the rest of the fudge, shoving pieces into their mouths, though they are sickened by it, and soon spit it out again. NADBO has a minor choking fit.)

MR.. *(With camera.)* O.K., guys! Everybody smile! Say "MON KEE!"

(MRS. embraces the children, smiling radiantly at the camera. The children cringe at the flash.)

MRS. This is the happiest day of my life. Thank you, God.

MR. This is the happiest day of my life. *(MR. hands X the camera so that he/she can take a picture of the new family. MR., MRS. smiling broadly, NABBO and NADBO cringing. NADBO tries to hide under the sweater, and MRS. gently removes it.)* Thanks!

X. *(Handing camera back to MR..)* Lovely. Now, we should complete our procedure. Your signatures, please—

MR., MRS. Yes, yes of course...

(Again, X draws the clipboard back out of their reach, at the crucial moment.)

X. Ummm—just a moment. *(Peering at a document)* I'm afraid— Nabbo and Nadbo have a third sibling.

MR. has taken the pen from X's hand, and now drops it.

MRS. *(Faint, hand to bosom.)* A third...?

MR.. ...another twin?

X. *(Hesitant.)* Not "twin" exactly. With these high-fertility races, the precise clinical term is—too clinical. Let's say "identical sibling."

MR. Tri-tri-triplets?

THE ADOPTION

X Not "triplets," exactly. *(Evasively.)* "Identical sibling" is preferred.

MRS. *(Vague, voice strange.)* Oooohhh another of you!—how, how—how wonderful.

(NABBO, NADBO poke each other, but do not speak. Cap bells jingle. One shoves at the shiny firetruck, or the wagon. The other finds a piece of fudge and pops it into his mouth.)

MR. *(Awkward, dazed, to X.)* B-But I'm afraid—we really can't, you know. Not three. We'd only prepared for one.

MRS. When we left home yesterday—to drive here—we'd only prepared—enough diapers, a single bassinet— *(Pause; a kind of wildness comes over her.)* A third? A third baby? Is it possible? I did always want a large family...

MR.. But, darling, not in five minutes!

MRS. We can buy a new house. More bedrooms! Bunkbeds! A bigger family room! *(Pause, breathing quickly.)* I was lonely in my parents' house—just the one of me. And everything done for me. Never a moment's want or deprivation... *(Pause.)* My mother was from a large family—eight children. Dozens of grandchildren.

MR. But not in five minutes!

MRS. *(Turning on him, cutting.)* What difference does that make? We've been infertile—sterile—for fourteen years. We've got a lot of catching up to do!

MR. *(Wincing.)* Thirteen years...

MRS. *(Laughing, trying to hug NABBO and NADBO.)* Here is our—deliverance! These "tragic orphans"—from the dark side of the Earth." Human beings can't live for themselves alone...

MR. *(Gripping MRS. by the shoulders.)* Darling, please! You're hysterical. You're not—yourself.

MRS. *(Shrilly.)* Who am I, then? Who am I, then?

MR. Darling!—

(NABBO and NADBO have been cringing fearfully.)

X. *(With authority.)* Mr.—, Mrs.—? I'm afraid your allotted time has nearly transpired. Even as you dally— *(X indicates the clock.)* —this past hour, 110,273 new tragic orphans" have been, as it's said, "born."

MRS. *(Hand to bosom.)* How many?—my goodness!

MR. I think we've been cruelly misled here. I strongly object to being manipulated!

THE ADOPTION

X. If you had troubled to read the agency's restrictions and guidelines handbook, Mr.—, more closely, you would not affect such surprise now.

MR. I did read it! I've practically memorized it! We've been on your damned waiting list for a decade!

MRS. *(Vague, intense, to X.)* There is a—a third sibling?—identical with our b-babies?

X. Identical DNA, chromosomes—identical faces and bodies. But, you know, not "identical" inwardly. In the soul.

MRS. "The soul—!" *(A strange expression on her face as of radiance, pain.)*

MR. *(Awkward, flush-faced.)* Darling, it's just that we—can't. We don't have room—

MRS. Of course we have room!

MR. We don't have resources—

MRS. Of course we have resources!

MR. *(Tugging at his necktie, panting.)* We're practically in debt— paupers—

MRS. *(Extravagantly, arms wide.)* We're wealthy!—we have infinite space—inwardly.

MR. Inwardly?

MRS. The soul is infinite, isn't it? Mine is, isn't yours?

MR. *(Baffled.)* My—soul? Where—?

MRS. *(Tugging at X's arm.)* You tell him! The soul is infinite, isn't it? "The kingdom of God is within"—space that goes on forever!

(MRS. has been working herself up into an emotional state; NABBO and
NADBO are frightened of her. They cast off the cap, sweater, etc., shove
away the tricycle; begin to make mournful keening sounds and rock
back and forth, their small bodies hunched. X scolds them inaudibly;
they make a break for the closed door, and X grabs their arms to stop
them.)

MRS. What?—where are you going? Nab-bo—no, you're Nad-bo—I mean Nab-do—Nab-boo—come here! be good! you're ours, aren't you? Mommy loves you so much— *(Tries to embrace children, who resist her.)*

MR. *(Blank, dazed smile.)* Daddy loves you so much! *(Pushes the tricycle back.)* Since the beginning if Time!

MRS. Since before the beginning of Time—

(NABBO and NADBO cower, hiding behind X, who is annoyed at the turn of

events, surreptitiously slapping at the children or gripping their shoulders forcibly. The mourning-keening sounds seem to be coming from all over.)

MRS. *(Hands to ears.)* Oh, what is that sound! It hurts my ears—

MR.. Nab-boo! Nad-doo! Bad boys! Stop that!

X. *(Threatening children.)* It's just some village dirge—nothing! Pay no attention!

MRS.: It's coming from here, too— *(Impulsively rushes to the door and opens it, steps through; X immediately pulls her back.)*

X. *(Furious.)* Mrs.—! This door can only be opened by authorized agency personnel! *(X shuts the door.)*

(MRS. has recoiled back into the room. Hand over her mouth, she staggers forward as if about to collapse.)

MR. *(Rushing to help her.)* Darling? What is it?

X. That door was not to be opened. I could call a security guard and have you arrested, Mrs.—! Taken out of here in handcuffs!

MRS.. *(Eyes shut, nauseated.)* Oh...oh...

MR. Darling, what did you see?

X . *(Loudly.)* Mrs.—saw nothing. There was nothing to be seen.

MR. Darling—?

MRS.. *(Feeble whisper, leaning on MR.'s arm.)* Take them back. We don't want them.

MR. What did you see, darling? What's behind that door?

MRS. *(Trying to control rising hysteria.)* Take them back. We don't want them. Any of them. I want to go home.

X. Hmmm! I thought so. Poor risks for adoption.

MR. Darling, are you certain? We've waited so long...prayed so long...

MRS.. *(A small scream.)* Take them away! All of them! *(Hides eyes.)* We're not strong enough—

X. *(Coldly.)* You're certain, Mr. and Mrs.—? You can never again apply with our agency, you know.

MRS. Take them away!

MR. *(Trying to speak in normal voice.)* We're sorry—so sorry—

(X marches NABBO and NADBO out, and the door is shut behind them.)

MR. *(Weakly, belatedly calling after.)* Um—so sorry—

THE ADOPTION

(The mourning-keening sound grows louder. MR. and MRS. freeze; LIGHTS DIM except on the clock face, where the minute hand continues its accelerated progress. LIGHTS OUT. MOURNING SOUND CEASES. LIGHTS UP on MR. and MRS., who have come forward. DARKNESS elsewhere. The clock is no longer visible. MR. and MRS. speak in a duet of fagitated rhythms, overlappings, a strange music that should suggest, though not too overtly mimic, the mourning-keening sound. This conclusion should be elegiac, a barely restrained hysteria; but it is restrained.)

MRS. *(Hands to her face.)* What have we done!—

MR.: It was a, a wise decision—

MRS.: —necessary—

MR.: —necessary decision—

MRS.: Waited all our lives— Oh, what have we done—

MR.: It was your decision—

MRS.: Our day of birth—delivery—

MR.: Deliverance—

MRS.: —weren't strong enough—

MR.: You weren't— I was— *(Pause.)* —wasn't—

MRS.: What have we done!—not strong enough—

MR.: Who the hell is strong enough I'd like to know—

MRS.: God didn't make us strong enough—

MR. —rational decision, necessary—

MRS. —necessary— *(Clutching at her womb.)* Oh! Oh what have we done! My babies—

MR.. *(Anguished, strikes chest with fist.)* I'm only human! What can I do! Who can forgive me? *(Pause, peers into audience.)* Who isn't human? You cast the first stone!

MRS. *(Hands framing face.)* That corridor!—that space!—to the horizon!—so many! And the smell. *(Nauseated.)*

MR.. *(Reasoning.)* There isn't room in the heart—I mean the home—the house!—no matter how many bunkbeds. We're not paupers!—I mean, we're not millionaires. Who's been saying we are?

MRS. *(Confused.)* Bunkbeds?—how many?

MR.. How many? *(Rapidly counting on fingers, confused.)*

MRS. *(A soft cry.)* Our home—house!—empty!—

MR. *(Protesting.)* Hey, there's us.

MRS. So lonely!—

THE ADOPTION

MR. Rational, necessary decision—no choice.

MRS. So lonely—

MR. Look, I refuse to be manipulated, to be made guilty—

MRS. So many years waiting, and so lonely—

MR. *(Pleading.)* Who the hell isn't human? I ask you!

MRS. *(Has found the knitted cap on the floor, picks it up lovingly, bells chime.)* God knows, God sees into the heart. Forgive us, God—

MR.. We had no choice.

MRS. —no choice!

MR. And we're not millionaires!

(Lights begin to fade.)

MRS. *(Waving, tearful and smiling.)* Goodbye Nabbo!—Nadbo!—Nabdo?—dear, innocent babies! Mommy loved you so!

MR. *(Waving, ghastly smile.)* Goodbye, boys! Sons! Your Daddy loved you so!

MRS. Don't think ill of us, don't forget us! Goodbye!

MR. Goodbye, sons! Be brave!

MRS. *(Blowing kisses.)* Mommy loved you so! Goodbye!

MR./MRS. Goodbye, goodbye, goodbye!

(Lights out.)

END OF PLAY

WHEN I WAS A LITTLE GIRL AND MY MOTHER DIDN'T WANT ME

(LIGHTS UP. An elderly woman speaks. Her voice alternates between urgency and bemusement; emotion and reflection.)

My father was killed and I never knew why.
Then, I was given away. By my mother.
I was so little...six months.
There were too many of us, nine of us,
    my mother gave me away.

When I was old enough to know...I cried a lot.
My father was killed and I never knew why.
No one would tell me.
Now there's no one I can ask.
"Why? Why?"
It happened in a fight, in a tavern, he was only
  forty-four years old.
My father I never Knew. Forty-four! Now, he could be
  my son.

I wasn't always an...old woman.   Eighty-one.
I was a girl for so long. I was a little girl for so long.
I was six months old when my father died.
And there were too many of us to feed, and my mother...
    gave me away.

There were nine children. I was the baby.
I was born late, I was the baby.
My mother gave me to her sister Lena who didn't have
    children. This was in 1918.
This was in the Black Rock section of Buffalo,
  the waterfront on the Niagara River.
Germans, Poles, Hungarians...immigrants.
We were Hungarians. We were called "Hunkies."
I don't know why people hated us...

WHEN I WAS A LITTLE GIRL AND
MY MOTHER DIDN'T WANT ME

(WOMAN pauses; decides not to explore this.)

Uncle John and Aunt Lena were my "parents."
We moved to a farm far away in the country.
And my real mother and my brothers and sisters moved to a farm a few miles away.
Uncle John and Aunt Lena were good to me.
I don't know if I loved them...I think I loved them. I think...
I think they loved me.
They wanted children but couldn't have them so it was
   right, I think, that my mother gave me to them... *(Pause)*
       it was a, a good thing, it was a... necessary thing.
I would learn one day that it happened often.
In immigrant families in those days.
In poor immigrant families.

My father was killed and I never knew why.
They said he was a bad drinker, he got drunk
       and was always in fights.
The Hungarians were the worst, they said—
       the drinking, and the fighting.
They said he was so handsome, my father.
My mother Elizabeth was so pratty.
Curly hair like mine.
They said he had a temper "like the devil."
In the tavern there was a fight, and he died.
A man took up a poker and beat my father to death.
I never knew why, I never knew who it had been.
Yet this was how my life was decided.

There is the moment of conception—you don't know.
There is the moment of birth—you don't know.
There is the moment your life is decided—you don't know.
Yet you say, "This is my life."
You say, "This is me."

*(WOMAN regards herself in wonder like a stroke victim regaining some of
       her awareness.)*

WHEN I WAS A LITTLE GIRL AND
MY MOTHER DIDN'T WANT ME

When I was a little girl and my mother didn't want me I hid away to cry.
I felt so bad and I felt so ashamed.
When I was old enough I would walk to the other farm.
There was a bridge over the Tonawanda Creek a few
    miles away.
They didn't really want to see me I guess.
My name was Carolina, but they didn't call me that.
I don't remember if there was a name they calles me.
They weren't very nice to me I guess.
They didn't want me, I guess I was a reminder of...
    something.

Elizabeth, my mother, never learned English.
She spoke Hungarian all her life.
She never learned to read. She never learned to drive
    a car.
My Aunt Lena never learned to drive, so the sisters
    didn't see much of each other.
They lived only a few miles apart, and were the only
    sisters of their family in America, but they didn't
    see much of each other.
That was how women were in the old days.
I loved my mother.
She was a short, plump woman.
Curly brown hair like mine.
People would say, "You look just like your momma!"
Then they would be surprised, I'd start to cry.
My mother scolded me in Hungarian—
"Go away, go home where you belong. You have a home.
Your home is not here."

I loved my big brothers and sisters.
There was Leslie, he was the oldest.
He took over when my father died.
There was Mary, I didn't get to know real well.
They were born in Budapest.
There was Steve, who'd been kicked and trampled
    by a horse. His brain was injured, he would never
    leave home.
There was Elsie who was my "big sister."

WHEN I WAS A LITTLE GIRL AND
MY MOTHER DIDN'T WANT ME

There was Frank who was my "big brother."
There was Johnny...and Edith...
There was George, I wasn't too close with George.
There was Joseph, I wasn't too close with.

(Pause)

They are all dead now.
I loved them, but...
I am the only one remaining.
Sometimes I think: The soul is just a burning match!
It burns a while and then...
And then that's all.

It's a long time ago now, but I remember hiding
away to cry.
When I was a little girl and my mother didn't want me.

END OF PLAY

SHORT PLAYS FOR EVERY VENUE

JUDGMENT CALL AND OTHER PLAYS
Frederick Stroppel

This collection of darkly comic one-acts by the author of *Single and Proud and Other Plays* includes *Judgment Call, Soulmates, Chain Mail, Perfect Pitch* and *Coelacanth.* (#12658)

ISRAEL HOROVITZ: 5 SHORT PLAYS

Free Gift, Speaking Well of the Dead, Three Weeks After Paradise, Security and *A Mother's Love,* five dramas written in the aftermath of September ll[th], are included this collection by the prolific American playwright. (#21973)

OFF-OFF BROADWAY FESTIVAL PLAYS / 27

Born to Be Blue by Mark Bellusci, *The Parrot* by Le Wilhelm, *Flights* by Susan Cameron, *A Doctor's Visit* by Mark Loewenstern, *Three Questions* by Maurice Martin and *The Devil's Parole* by Eric Giancoli were winners in the 27th Annual Short Play Festival. (#17706)

THE KUKKURRIK FABLES
Oscar Mandel

Forty-two playlets for two to ten actors combine wisdom and whimsy for auditions, show fillers or full evenings of Aesop-like tales with a modern twist. (#13060)

SHADOWBOXING
The Shadowbox Cabaret Theatre

Twenty-two outrageous sketches provide an eclectic mix of comic gems, some of the most successful material ever performed at the renowned Columbus cabaret. (#21461)

TEN-MINUTE PLAYS FROM
ACTORS THEATRE OF LOUISVILLE /Volume 5
Edited by Michael Bigelow Dixon and Michele Volansky
Foreword by Jon Jory

Twenty-five short plays by some of the most exciting dramatists writing today are included in this volume. The series is popular for classes and showcases. (#22275)

For the broadest selection of short plays in print, see
THE BASIC CATALOGUE OF PLAYS AND MUSICALS
online at www.samuelfrench.com

SHORT PLAYS FOR EVERY VENUE

THE BEQUEST by Dale Wasserman
Eyebrows rise in a small town when a notorious playboy dies leaving a large bequest to the lovely wife of a local reporter. "A polished miniature from a playwright better known for his blockbusters."—*What's On*. 3 m., 3 f.(#4267)

CELEBRATION by Harold Pinter
Diners and the staff at an elegant restaurant treat audiences to some unusually entertaining fare in this London hit by a major voice of the modern theatre. "[An] entire smorgasbord of gorgeous verbal moves."—*New Yorker*. 5 m., 4 f. (#5870)

THE JUICE OF WILD STRAWBERRIES
by Jean Lenox Toddie
A woman seeks renewal after loss in this touching play. "This gem celebrates life, love and the wisdom that comes with age."—Mill Mountain Theatre, Roanoke. 1 m., 1 f. (#12659)

MOSQUITO DIRIGIBLE AEROSOL DEODORANT
by Conrad E. Davidson
A professor who thinks he is a dirigible undergoes other transformations during therapy, even becoming a mosquito. Unfortunately, the psychiatrist has an obsessive fear ... of mosquitoes. 2 m., 2 f. (#15732)

REFUGEES by Stephanie Satie
The hearts and minds of new immigrants and refugees as they reinvent their lives in American are revealed in five scenes that are set over five weeks in an English as a Second Language class. 1 f. (to play 3 m., 7 f.) (#19773)

SLAVERY by Jonathan Payne
In the 1030's, the Federal Writer's Project interviewed former slaves who were then in their eighties, nineties and older. Here are some of these moving, first-hand narratives. Paired with traditional Negro spirituals, they offer dramatic insights into the human side of slavery. 3 m., 4 f. (#21521)

For the broadest selection of short plays in print, see
THE BASIC CATALOGUE OF PLAYS AND MUSICALS